At Issue

S0-BBY-120

White Supremacy Groups

Other Books in the At Issue Series:

Alcohol Abuse

Bulimia

Can Diets Be Harmful?

Child Athletes

Date Rape

Does Capital Punishment Deter Crime?

Drunk Driving

Extreme Sports

Homeschooling

Human Embryo Experimentation

Islamic Fundamentalism

Organ Transplants

Pandemics

Policing the Internet

Political Activism

Private Character in the Public Eye

Sexually Transmitted Diseases

Should College Athletes Be Paid?

Should the United States Move to Electronic Voting?

User-Generated Content

Volunteerism

What Are the Causes of Prostitution?

What Is a Hate Crime?

Will the World Run Out of Fresh Water?

At Issue

White Supremacy Groups

Mitchell Young, Book Editor

GREENHAVEN PRESS

An imprint of Thomson Gale, a part of The Thomson Corporation

THOMSON

GALE

Detroit • New York • San Francisco • New Haven, Conn. • Waterville, Maine • London

Christine Nasso, *Publisher*
Elizabeth Des Chenes, *Managing Editor*

© 2008 The Gale Group.

Star logo is a trademark and Gale and Greenhaven Press are registered trademarks used herein under license.

For more information, contact:
Greenhaven Press
27500 Drake Rd.
Farmington Hills, MI 48331-3535
Or you can visit our Internet site at http://www.gale.com

LIBRARY OF CONGRESS CATALOGING-IN-PUBLICATION DATA

White supremacy groups / Mitchell Young, book editor.
   p. cm. -- (At issue)
  Includes bibliographical references and index.
  ISBN-13: 978-0-7377-3699-1 (hardcover)
  ISBN-13: 978-0-7377-3700-4 (pbk.)
  1. White supremacy movements. 2. Hate groups. 3. Racism. I. I. Young, Mitchell.
  HS1610.W55 2008
  320.5'6--dc22

                                        2007036330

ISBN-10: 0-7377-3699-2 (hardcover)
ISBN-10: 0-7377-3700-X (pbk.)

Printed in the United States of America
10 9 8 7 6 5 4 3 2 1

Contents

Introduction   **7**

1. White Americans Must Build   **10**
Separate Communities
John Hunt Morgan

2. In an Era of Racial Revolution,   **17**
Whites Need to Regain Group Solidarity
Sam Francis

3. Nationalist Parties Defend European   **28**
Culture Against Immigrant Attack
Kyle Rogers

4. The Belgian Nationalist Party Promotes   **36**
Extremism and Xenophobia
Angus Roxburgh

5. Whites Feel Threatened by the Booming   **41**
Hispanic Population
Roberto Lovato

6. Hardcore Racists Exploit Concern Over   **47**
Immigration to Gain Recruits
Chip Berlet

7. Whites Should Work Together to Advance   **53**
Their Interests
Jamie Glazov and Jared Taylor

8. The New White Supremacists Mask Racism   **59**
with Pseudo-Intellectualism
Dennis Roddy

9. Women Play a Subordinate but Vital Role   **65**
in White Supremacist Groups
Kathleen M. Blee

10. Women are Gaining Leadership Roles   76
    in White Nationalist Organizations
    Lisa Turner with Russ Nieli

11. Behind an Innocent Facade White   83
    Supremacist Singers Spread Hate
    Earl Ofari Hutchinson

12. Christian Identity's Bizarre Beliefs   87
    Lead to Extreme Violence
    Anti-Defamation League

13. White Racialists Should Lead   94
    Honorable White Lives
    Robert S. Griffin

Organizations to Contact   103
Bibliography   108
Index   113

Introduction

In the past twenty years, a new type of white supremacist group has emerged. Sometimes referring to themselves as "white nationalists," their members distance themselves from the violent image of their predecessors. Group members are more likely to be seen in a business suit debating issues than wearing robes at a cross burning. Some groups present themselves as ethnic activist organizations, asserting that they are only looking out for the interests of whites, just as other groups look out for the interests of African Americans and Hispanics. Other white supremacist groups seek to separate themselves from other races, forming all or overwhelmingly white communities. Still other organizations do not advocate any particular program, but serve as forums for like-minded individuals to gather, debate, and socialize.

A major effort of these new groups is to educate (critics would say propagandize) the public as to their point of view. One of the chief voices putting out the new white supremacist line is Jared Taylor, the editor of *American Renaissance* magazine. Taylor, fluent in Japanese and French, with degrees from Columbia University and the Sorbonne (France), has often appeared on radio talk shows in order to promote his views. He also holds a biennial *American Renaissance* conference, where participants are required to wear a jacket and tie. Critics claim that he is deceitful, billing himself as a "race-relations expert" when he is just dressing up old-fashioned hatred. They joke that if not for the suit and tie requirement, meeting attendees would show up in Nazi regalia.

Taylor responds that he is merely stating unpleasant facts—such as the difference between races in crime rates or the tendency for even white liberals to segregate themselves in mostly white neighborhoods—that others prefer to ignore. Taylor claims that he is not advocating an "all white America" or return of segregation. Rather, he believes that "people prefer the company of people like themselves, that this is natural and healthy, and that we should organize our society on this assumption." The two policies he advocates are "the repeal of all anti-discrimination laws and an end to immigration." Taylor believes that if these policies were implemented, most people would naturally self-segregate.

Lynx and Lamb Gaede, the teenage girls of the musical duo Prussian Blue, are at the opposite end of the age spectrum from Jared Taylor and appeal to a completely different audience. The two sing pop music that is designed to reflect "white pride," instilling in its listeners a sense of heritage they believe is common in other groups but is prohibited to white folks. "We're proud of being white, we want to keep being white," Lynx was quoted in an ABC News story. What Prussian Blue and Jared Taylor have in common is that they are seeking new ways of reaching a larger group of white people. They are promoting a message they believe many, if not most, whites in America would agree with if it weren't for the bias in the major media against advocacy for whites.

This is particularly true when it comes to the issue of immigration. White nationalist groups fear that immigration of non-whites into the United States will have disastrous consequences for whites. Furthermore, they note that all Western industrial countries are admitting large numbers of non-white immigrants, not just the traditionally immigrant friendly United States. In some Northern European cities, the indigenous population is outnumbered by recent immigrants and their children, while in the United States, whites have dropped from over 80 percent of the population to about two thirds in the course of thirty years. Uneasiness about immigration is not limited to white supremacists, however. A June 2007 Gallup Poll found that 45 percent of Americans wanted to see the level of immigration into the country decrease, compared to 35 percent who approved of the current level. This concern about immigration has given the new white nationalist groups an opportunity to reach a broader audience than might otherwise have been the case.

Critics warn that Americans should not be fooled, that these new white supremacists are simply repackaging hate, using fear of change and xenophobia to encouraging discrimination and even violence against nonwhites. One of Jared Taylor's critics, the anti-racist activist and author Tim Wise, notes that Taylor has allowed neo-Nazis and those who advocate violence to attend conferences sponsored by *American Renaissance*, Taylor's journal. According to Wise, "Taylor refuses to turn Nazis away from his conferences, preferring to take their money and have them in attendance."

Wise believes that even when whites slip into minority status, they will maintain their traditional privileges in the United States. He notes that Asian and African American groups have maintained their cultural identity despite being relatively small minorities historically. According to Wise, whites have nothing to fear from the changing demographics of the United States. In contrast, author Peter Brimelow, who operates the immigration restriction advocacy site *Vdare.com*, believes it is "inevitable that as whites become a minority in the United States, they will act like other minorities and form activist groups to promote their ethnic interests." Only time will tell who is correct. But it is already clear that—by attempting to disassociate themselves in the public's mind from violent racist organizations and capitalizing on concerns over immigration and other issues—new model white supremacist organizations are getting their message to a broad audience.

1

White Americans Must Build Separate Communities

John Hunt Morgan

John Hunt Morgan is the pen-name for a racially conscious author.

White families need an environment peopled by others like them. A step toward this goal is home schooling children, but this is not enough. Racially conscious whites must seek to establish communities in which they control the local government. They will then be able to create, without violence, overwhelmingly white communities in which their children can thrive.

How can we give our children a proper start in life? In the October 2001 issue of *AR* [*American Renaissance*] there is an excellent article about rearing honorable white children. [Professor] Robert Griffin of the University of Vermont profiled a number of families that have taken their racial responsibilities seriously, and who have arranged their households so as to instill sound racial and cultural values. These are inspiring stories, and the children will no doubt benefit greatly. However, these families all did something not all families can do: They taught their children at home rather than send them to school.

Home schooling is, of course, the only way to control what children learn, but not every family can do it. Even if an adult is home all day, not all parents or children are tempera-

John Hunt Morgan, "Building White Communities," *American Renaissance*, vol. 15, no. 11, November 2004. www.amren.com. Reproduced by permission.

mentally suited to home schooling. Also, a single, self-contained family is not a community. Children need playmates.

A Healthy Atmosphere for Whites

What would be ideal is a place where the neighbors think as we do, and where the school teachers, the mayor, and the fire chief do, too. We need a community of racially conscious whites who build—simply by being together—the healthy atmosphere whites used to take for granted.

As a father, I am particularly conscious of the benefits such a community would have for children, but it would have great benefits for adults, too. How pleasant it would be for a neighborhood get-together to feel like an *American Renaissance* conference. At the last conference I attended, someone said to me, "It's great to be among the living again." It would be wonderful to *live* among the living.

The most important aspect of such a community would be the education it offered children. Any group that is out of step with the mainstream in any fundamental way—and, for the time being, racially conscious whites are radically out of step—must be able to rear children in a way that supports dissident thinking.

> *[The Amish] have been very successful in preserving a way of life completely at odds with the rest of America.*

Would it be difficult to gather together the nucleus of such a community? Certainly it would, but it would be easier than electing a racially healthy Congress or state legislature. At the same time, even a small zone of healthy white consciousness could become a base for efforts at achieving larger changes. Sooner or later, whites will form communities of their own, and the sooner we begin, the more successful we will be.

Communities Have to Be Built

Communities of like-minded people do not spring up by accident. People have to build them, and Americans have a long history of building them. Most such people, like the Amish and the Shakers and Mormons, have had religious motives, but Americans have gathered for all kinds of reasons, some of them completely harebrained. Until recently, a black man named Dwight York, a convicted rapist who claimed to have come from the planet Rizq, ran the United Nuwaubian Nation of Moors at a compound not far from Eatonton, Georgia. One hundred fifty Nuwaubians lived at the site, practicing an odd mixture of invented and Egyptian religion. They would still be there if it had not come to light that Mr. York was molesting little Nuwaubian girls.

If state regulations demanded teaching units on American Indians, the slave trade, or American multiculturalism, these subjects could certainly be taught—though from a more traditional point of view.

An even more extreme example was Jim Jones and his Peoples Temple. He managed to get more than 900 people to move to Guyana and build a town in which they could practice their religion. They built a system to train members in their dissident views, but it began to unravel, and on Nov. 18, 1978, they all committed suicide. The point here is that even crazy people can leave their old lives and build communities. Sane white people should certainly be able to do considerably better.

Probably the best-known example of a group that has built its own institutions to maintain a sharply dissident way of life is the Amish. [The Amish are a religious sect descended from German-speaking settlers who reject most modern technology and devices.] They have been very successful in preserving a way of life completely at odds with the rest of

America, but they are not a good model for racially conscious whites. They have farm communities that have been established, in some cases, for centuries. Most racially conscious whites are not farmers, and they need to form new communities, not carry on the ones into which they were born.

The Amish also have an unusual education system. They study in private, one-room schools that go up only to 8th grade. The Amish and Mennonites received a special Supreme Court exemption in 1972 from state requirements for education beyond middle school, successfully arguing that their people learn wisdom in the household and behind the plow, and that secondary schools are purveyors of temptation and worldliness. Racially conscious whites have the same distrust of high schools, but most would rather fix them than abolish them.

The Importance of Schools

The school system is the key to a successful community. Children cannot sustain a dissident point of view in the face of a school system that teaches liberal nonsense. Orthodox Jews have always understood this, and because their schools are religious they have built private schools to sustain their way of life.

Private schools for whites are desirable but not necessary. Setting one up is a big job, and with enough people in a community, it would be easier and cheaper to elect a school board, and revamp the public schools. American schools teach the same subjects they did 50 years ago. It is the emphasis that has shifted, and there is no reason why a racially conscious school could not shift the emphasis back. A curriculum taken unchanged from 50 years ago probably would be, except for a few odds and ends like sex education, in compliance with current standards. If state regulations demanded teaching units on American Indians, the slave trade, or American multiculturalism, these subjects could certainly be taught—though from a more traditional point of view. In fact, it would be important to cover those subjects thoroughly whether they were required or not. Any child who went to college after an education of this kind might be in for a shock, but by that age healthy ideas would probably be unassailable.

There are now more than enough racially aware whites to move gradually into a small town and remake its institutions. These whites would not have to be a majority in order to elect town councilmen or school board members. An activist minority can achieve a great deal, and any largely white town would have a certain number of original inhabitants who would support a return to good sense.

As soon as a town had a reputation for white consciousness, no non-whites would want to live there.

Where to Go?

The question, of course, is where whites should go. Moving is a great bother, and everyone can think of reasons why the best place for a white community is the place where he already lives. Some obvious criteria are that if an existing town is to be taken over, it should be small, already overwhelmingly white, and with its own small school district. If a school is part of a huge, county-wide school district, for example, it could not be returned to sanity without taking over the entire district—an extremely difficult undertaking.

After people move, they have to make a living. It would be important to choose a town not far from a metropolitan area with jobs. When the Orthodox [Jewish] congregations built new towns, they arranged for private commuter buses into New York City so people could support themselves. It would be good to attract a certain number of retired people whose pension or Social Security income would follow them wherever they moved. A retirement home in a white town would be attractive to older people who prefer to be looked after by people from the community rather than by black and Puerto Rican orderlies.

Some would fear that the government would make it impossible to run a white town, but I disagree. Sooner or later it would become clear what was happening, but no laws *require* residential integration, and the country is still largely segregated. As soon as a town had a reputation for white consciousness, no non-whites would want to live there. If a few insisted on moving in as test cases, they would have to be let in; there could be no outright discrimination. However, no one wants to spend his life as a test case. Such people would move in with great fanfare, but would soon move out. If a certain number of non-whites decided to stay, they would have to be tolerated. Very few would choose that kind of life, and a handful of odd-balls would be a small price to pay for a healthy-minded community. The town would have to be very careful never to break anti-discrimination laws, but practically everything necessary for a real white community can be achieved entirely within the law.

Great Things from Modest Beginnings

Some might argue that starting small in this way is a renunciation of the larger, national goals of a white consciousness movement. On the contrary, it could well be that only modest beginnings can lead to greater achievements. A successful white community would grow. It could become the nucleus for a region that would send representatives to the state house and to Washington. The region would not only have a political voice, it would inspire imitators.

In the February 1995 issue of *AR* there was a debate about whether the United States could be saved as a unitary, white state or whether whites would have to accept partition if they are to gain a homeland. This was an interesting but entirely abstract debate that does nothing to solve the problems we face every day. White communities are compatible with either approach—partition or unitary state—and have the immeasurable advantage of large benefits now. Small gatherings of whites will not immediately change the government in Washington or detoxify the national media, but they would be the beginnings of a real, practical movement to save our race and culture. Let us begin to cultivate our corners of the world even as we work to change it.

2

In an Era of Racial Revolution, Whites Need to Regain Group Solidarity

Sam Francis

The late Sam Francis, who held a Ph.D. in history from the University of North Carolina, wrote for the Washington Times *and later for VDARE.com.*

Race is a biological fact and a political reality. It is natural for whites to wish to preserve their culture and their biological uniqueness. Historically, whites have banded together to preserve their political power. Since the civil rights revolution, however, other races fought for their own well-being, while whites have attempted to be racially neutral. This creates a dangerous situation for whites, because their political leaders refuse to protect the interests of whites in the face of demands for programs such as affirmative action. Separation is the preferable long-term solution to the inevitable conflicts caused by a multiracial society.

[The White] Race today faces a crisis that within the coming century and in the United States and Europe could easily lead to either its physical extinction, its subordination to and persecution by other races, or the destruction of its civilization.

Most readers who continue to believe what the dominant culture tells them about the meaning and significance of race will find this concern bizarre. Even if race does exist as a bio-

Sam Francis, "Introduction: The Return of the Repressed," *Race and the American Prospect: Essays on the Racial Realities of Our Nation and Our Time*, ed. Sam Francis, Mt. Airy, MD: Occidental Press, 2006, pp. 1–20. Reproduced by permission.

logical reality, it certainly has no meaning for behavior, culture, intelligence, or other traits that influence and shape social institutions. Moreover, any effort to take race more seriously is either a deliberate and covert attempt to justify racial hatred or injustice, or is at best a misguided enterprise that is all too likely to lead to hatred, injustice, and even genocide, as it has in the past. This is the conventional attitude toward race that the dominant culture in the West today promotes and enforces. . . .

Race Is a Biological and Political Reality

The commonly held beliefs about race mentioned above—that it does not exist or is not important and that serious concern about race and racial identity leads to negative and undesirable consequences—are wrong. Yet it is precisely those beliefs that make it impossible for whites who accept them to preserve themselves as a race and the civilization and political institutions their race has created. As black historian Shelby Steele acknowledged in the *Wall Street Journal* (November 13, 2003), "Racial identity is simply forbidden to whites in America and across the entire Western world. Black children today are hammered with the idea of racial identity and pride, yet racial pride in whites constitutes a grave evil. Say 'I'm white and I'm proud' and you are a Nazi." Indeed, he made use of the widely shared (by nonwhites as well as whites) demonic view of whites to reject and deny any white claim to their own racial identity:

> No group in recent history has more aggressively seized power in the name of its racial superiority than Western whites. This race illustrated for all time—through colonialism, slavery, white racism, Nazism—the extraordinary human evil that follows when great power is joined to an atavistic sense of superiority and destiny.

[African American leaders] Louis Farrakhan, Al Sharpton, and Jesse Jackson, as well as Hispanic leaders Cruz Bustamante and Mario Obledo, have no problem exulting in their own racial identity and the political power they expect such solidarity to yield. They exult in language that is explicitly anti-white, in the most primitive and threatening terms. Yet they are seldom called to account for it. When Mr. Obledo, proclaimed a few years ago, "California is going to be a Mexican state, we are going to control all the institutions. If people don't like it they should leave—go back to Europe," he received the Presidential Medal of Freedom by President Clinton soon afterward. It is not very likely that a white leader today who said, as Illinois Senator Stephen Douglas in a debate with Abraham Lincoln in 1858 did say, "I believe this government was made on the white basis. I believe it was made by white men for the benefit of white men and their posterity forever" would be awarded anything. Douglas's comment (and many similar ones) expressed a sentiment more or less parallel to Mr. Obledo's, though Douglas did not go so far as to invite nonwhites to leave the country (it was Lincoln himself who did that). Douglas in fact won the election and was the Democrat's national candidate for president two years later.

In contrast to Mr. Obledo, when Senate Majority Leader Trent Lott in December 2002 remarked that the country would have been better off had Strom Thurmond won the 1948 presidential election [Thurmond ran on an anti-civil-rights platform], he was denounced from both the political right and left and hounded into resigning his leadership position in the U.S. Senate. Mr. Lott had said nothing about race, and there was no evidence he was even thinking about that aspect of the campaign [the comment was made at a 100th birthday party for Thurmond], but he was obliged to engage in protracted and repeated retractions, anyway—all to no avail.

A Racial Double Standard

One main reason for the obvious double standard is that nonwhites are easily inflamed and mobilized by the slightest appearance of white identity, and their mobilization can have disastrous consequences for institutions—the Republican Party—that seek or depend on nonwhite votes or market patronage. Yet these are by no means the only reasons why whites "cannot openly have a racial identity."

The truth is that whites deny themselves a racial identity.

The truth is that whites deny themselves a racial identity. Mr. Steele can utter sweeping generalizations about "the extraordinary human evil" (ignoring the long and brutal history of slavery, conquest, genocide, and repression by nonwhites in Africa and Asia that persist to this day) in a major newspaper owned and managed by whites because most of the white elite will not question this kind of anti-white opinion. White tolerance of such anti-white sentiment is due to the guilt that is injected into white minds. . . .

White leaders no doubt assume that the multiracial future of the country will not threaten whites or the country because all races accept or are coming to reject race in the same ways they do. This assumption is demonstrably wrong. Like most revolutions, the one led by nonwhites like Martin Luther King, Jr. moved from a moderate phase demanding merely equal treatment and the end of legal racial discrimination to a far more radical stage demanding outright racial privileges for nonwhites. It is this radical phase that established now that threatens to become even more radical.

Denying Biology

"Color blindness" denies a biological reality that is obviated in two ways. First, scientifically: The work of scientists like Arthur Jensen, William Shockley, J. Philippe Rushton, H. J. Eysenck, Richard Lynn, Richard Hernstein and a number of others established that race exists and is a significant factor in human mental traits. There is little doubt about this today and fewer and fewer scientists dispute it, though few also are willing to risk their careers by talking or writing about it. As long ago as 1981, [psychologist] Arthur Jensen itemized a host of such differences:

> Different races have evolved in somewhat different ways, making for many differences among them. A few of the many physical characteristics found to display genetic variation between different races are body size and proportions, hair form and distribution, head shape and facial features, cranial capacity and brain formation, blood types, number of vertebrae, size of genitalia, bone density, fingerprints, basic metabolic rate, body temperature, blood pressure, heat and cold tolerance, number and distribution of sweat glands, odor, consistency of ear wax, number of teeth, age at eruption of permanent teeth, fissural patterns on the surfaces of the teeth, length of gestation period, frequency of twin births, male-female birth ratio, physical maturity at birth, rate of infant development of alpha brain waves, colorblindness, visual and auditory acuity, intolerance of milk, galvanic skin resistance, chronic diseases, susceptibility to infectious diseases, genetic diseases (e.g., Tay-Sachs, sickle cell anemia), and pigmentation of the skin, hair, and eyes. . . .

Nonwhites may indeed create a different civilization of their own, but it will not be the same as the one we as whites created and live in, and most of us would not want to live in it.

[R]acial differences in intelligence and behavior patterns significantly affect such societal differences as levels of technological achievement, political stability and freedom, criminal violence, and standards of living. What kind of society and how much civilization a people creates, is clearly related to their race. Race by itself is certainly not sufficient to create civilization, but it is necessary to creating it. Nonwhites may indeed create a different civilization of their own, but it will not be the same as the one we as whites created and live in, and most of us would not want to live in it.

Recognition of Race Is Not "Hate"

The recognition of the significance of race does not imply or lead to "hate" or domination of one race by another, but racial differentiation does imply social differentiation. The existence of significant biological differences between groups of human beings means there will be social differences between them: differences in educational and economic achievement, personal and political behavior, and social and cultural institutions. And if there is social differentiation between races, then competition and conflict between them is also likely, especially if they occupy the same territory. "Hatred," domination, and racial antagonism may therefore result, not as relationships to be desired or advocated, but as the consequence of the natural reality of racial differences and the effort to ignore or deny such differences.

The second way in which race has been rediscovered is as a socio-political force, the racial consciousness and solidarity discussed above that in the last century has swept through the nonwhite populations of the United States and the world. This rediscovery constitutes what Lothrop Stoddard in the frank language of the 1920s called "The Rising Tide of Color against White World Supremacy" and is identical to what the late Robert Nisbet termed the "racial revolution." The "single fact . . . that stands out" is "that racial revolution as an aspiration is becoming increasingly separate from other philosophies or strategies of revolution."

What has occurred in the last century, then, consists of two processes—first, the evisceration of white racial consciousness and identity, and second, the development, around the same time, of the nonwhite and anti-white racial consciousness that animates the emerging national nonwhite majority. The scientific rediscovery of race as a socially and historically significant reality of nature is part of a reaction against the "racial revolution" and can be expected to assist in the revival and relegitimization of white racial identity, but remains largely an academic abstraction understood by only a handful of scientists and scholars.

[W]e now know enough about the biologically grounded cognitive and behavioral differences between the races to be able to say with confidence that race deeply affects and shapes cultural life.

The Necessity of White Racial Consciousness

There are three general reasons why a revival of white racial consciousness and identity is needed.

- First, we now know enough about the biologically grounded cognitive and behavioral differences between the races to be able to say with confidence that race deeply affects and shapes cultural life. Races with a lower level of cognitive capacity could have produced neither the modern West, with its scientific and technological achievements, nor the ancient West, with its vast political organization and sophisticated artistic and philosophical legacies. Nor is the inclinations of white Westerners to innovate, explore, expand, and conquer apparent among most nonwhite races, even if their cognitive capacities are greater than those of whites.

- Second, whites, like any race, should wish to survive and flourish simply for their own sake whatever their merits or flaws. Even this minimal rationale for racial survival is denied to whites today because of their constant demonization.

- And third, white racial consciousness is necessary simply as a means of self-protection. It is an integral component of the historic identity of America as a culture and a nation. . . . Explicit white racial consciousness has been commonplace and important feature of American history, a belief that has shaped the events, leaders, institutions, and norms that have defined us as a people and a nation throughout our past and in all regions.

You cannot have it both ways: either you define the American nation as the product of its past and learn to live with the reality of race of the racial particularism that in part defines our national history, or you reject race as meaningful and demand that anyone who believes that race means anything more than that be demonized. If you reject race, then you reject America as it has really existed throughout its history, and whatever you mean by "America" has to come from something other than its real past.

[T]he absence of racial consciousness among whites disarms them as a group in confrontation with races that possess such a consciousness.

Disarming Whites

Even more dangerously, the absence of racial consciousness among whites disarms them as a group in confrontation with races that possess such a consciousness. Blacks, Hispanics, Asians, and other nonwhite racial and ethnic groups are able to act and react in highly unified patterns, political and cultural. They protect what their leaders perceive as their racial interests and, in particular, to resist, denounce, and attack any manifestation of white racial solidarity.

Whites may be more or less unified with respect to objective material characteristics—income, education, residence, voting behavior, etc.—but they are not unified and indeed barely even exist with respect to racial consciousness and identity. At a time when anti-white racial and ethnic groups define themselves in explicitly racial terms, only our own unity and identity as a race will be able to meet their challenge. If and when that challenge should triumph and those enemies come to kill us as Robert Mugabe has threatened to do to whites in Zimbabwe, they will do so not because we are "Americans" or "Christians" or "conservatives" or "liberals," but because we are white.

Given the intensity of nonwhite racial consciousness, the emergence of a counterbalancing white consciousness may well lead to violent conflict between the races. There is in fact an immense level of violent conflict against whites going on right now through interracial crime and terrorism; by mass immigration, legal and illegal; and by the deliberate refusal of ruling white elites to enforce their own laws and protect their own people.

[Whites] can at least work to achieve results that would protect or guarantee their own survival and that of their civilization.

Possible Solutions

The restoration of white racial supremacy in the United States today is not desirable or probably even most possible. . . . The core of Robert E. Lee's [a leading general of the Confederacy during the Civil War] personal objection to Southern slavery was that it encouraged the corruption of the whites, a corruption that cripples and weakens whites in creating free social orders and high civilizations. A race that dominates needs to establish what is essentially an authoritarian system of political and social control that inhibits the dominant race almost as much as it restrains the subject race.

Probably the most desirable and mutually satisfactory (if not the most likely) resolution of the escalating racial conflict would be the voluntary separation of races into distinct nations. There are obvious problems with such a division of the national territory—who would get which part, what would happen to those of one race who refused to leave the areas assigned to another race, who would be counted as part of a race and why, how would the separation be authorized, how would each section be governed, etc. Moreover, most white Americans would recoil from endorsing an actual territorial division of the nation for whatever reason. Racial separatism, far more than "white supremacy," is today favored by most whites advocating white racial consciousness, but there appears to be little prospect of the larger white population embracing it in the near future. Nor is "racial federalism," under which local communities or even whole stales determine their own racial arrangements, laws, and policies, likely. The insistence by nationally dominant elites that race and immigration policies that are effectively anti-white be determined entirely by the centralized state under their own control means that localism and federalism are no more probable in race relations than in most other areas of American public life.

A Program for Survival

Nevertheless, if whites cannot expect a total, permanent, and mutually satisfactory resolution of the racial conflict through separation or federalism, they can at least work to achieve results that would protect or guarantee their own survival and that of their civilization. The political, legal, and cultural agenda on which whites should insist includes a permanent moratorium on all legal immigration into the United States, the expulsion of illegal aliens, the rigorous enforcement of laws against illegal immigration, and the removal of incentives to further illegal immigration (e.g., availability of welfare, education, and affirmative action for illegal aliens and of automatic birthright citizenship for their children); the end of all "affirmative action" programs and policies and of all "civil rights" laws that discriminate against whites and circumscribe their constitutional rights of association; the repeal of all "hate crime" laws and "Politically Correct" policies and regulations that penalize the peaceful expression of white racial consciousness and identity; and the abolition of all multiculturalist curricula, "sensitivity training," and similar experiments in brainwashing in schools, universities, businesses, and government. At the same time whites must seek to rebuild their own institutions—schools, businesses, churches, media, etc.—in which their own heritage and identity as whites can be preserved, honored, and transmitted to their descendants, and they must encourage measures that will help raise their own birth rates to at least replacement levels. Even these policies, however, would pit racially conscious whites against the dominant elites that continue to demand white racial dispossession and their non-white allies. Moreover, none of these measures will be adopted unless and until white racial consciousness is far more developed than it is today. Neither conventional conservative nor liberal ideologues show any serious interest in these particular measures or the racial identity they reflect, nor do either of the major political parties.

3

Nationalist Parties Defend European Culture Against Immigrant Attack

Kyle Rogers

Kyle Rogers is a board member of the Council of Conservative Citizens and webmaster of the organization's Web site. The Council is a U.S. activist group that is opposed to racial mixing and believes the United States should be a white, Christian nation.

The demographics of Europe are changing because of immigration from Africa and Asia. Reaction against immigration has increased the vote of nationalist parties. One party in particular has been successful, the Vlaams Belang *of Belgium. This party not only opposes immigration, but seeks to represent the Flemish speaking population in the country's northern half, called Flanders. (The people of the country's southern region, Walloonia, speak French). Vlaams Belang's ultimate goal is independence for Flanders, as well as a halt to immigration. Only the unscrupulous actions of the ruling Socialists have kept Vlaams Belang from power.*

A recent study conducted by Harvard University on multiculturalism drew the conclusion that "diversity has a corrosive effect on the community." No greater contemporary evidence exists than the rapid decline of many of Europe's iconic cities during the past few decades. Cities that withstood

Kyle Rogers, "Vlaams Belang and the Rise of European Nationalism," *Citizen Informer/ Council of Conservative Citizens Newsletter*, October 2006, pp. 16–17, 22. www.cofcc.org/citizeninformer. Reproduced by permission.

hundreds of years of wars can't withstand a couple decades non-European immigration.

Violent Clashes

In France 2,500 police officers were wounded during the first ten months of 2006 in violent clashes with immigrants, mostly Islamic, from northern and central Africa. Michel Thooris, law enforcement union head in France stated, "we are in a state of civil war, orchestrated by radical Islamists." Thooris advocates using armored personnel careers in immigrant ghettos instead of police cruisers. France has weekly race riots with sometimes hundreds of cars torched in a single week. During the nation-wide French student protest in March of 2006, thousands of immigrants poured out of the ghettos to beat and rob the as-sembled masses of college students. In numerous video tapes, rioters are heard shouting "Allah Akbar," and other Islamic cries while they carry out arsons, looting, and beatings.

In much of Europe, socialism and multi-culturalism are state religions with serious criminal penalties for political her-esy. Fortunately there are many who have fought back against the suicidal regimes in Europe. In almost every European country there is a new breed of political machinery that in-tends to save Western civilization. New parties have risen which oppose immigration, particularly non-European immi-gration that dilutes the national character and creates welfare states. Usually these parties are culturally conservative, popu-list, and nationalistic. They are generally referred to as Europe's "far-right."

Nationalism in Eastern Europe

In Eastern Europe, the so-called "far right" is much stronger than in Western Europe. In fact, one country recently saw a major upset. In the 2005 parliamentary elections, the socialist/liberal coalition that controlled Poland was totally crushed in just one election. Two conservative parties, including the hard-line Law & Order Party that came in first place, took a combined total of 51% of the vote. These parties formed a ruling coalition with the Self-Defense Party of Poland, which came in third place. This third party is socialist, but with culturally conservative values. The Self-Defense Party of Poland, refers to itself as the "Patriotic Left," and has counterparts in countries like Russia, Slovakia, and Eastern Germany. For example, Germany has two-right wing populist parties with seats in state parliaments in former East Germany. Whenever the right-wing parties poll high, some socialist candidates will come out against immigration to steal their main issue.

[The nationalist party] Vlaams Blok calls for the complete 'reversal of erroneous multi-cultural policies.

Poland stands out for another reason as well. Poland has had the most success in raising its native birthrate using government incentives. Countries like Germany and Slovakia are attempting to emulate Poland's success.

Surge in Western Europe

The situation in Western Europe is not so rosy, however. With massive numbers of non-European immigrants, draconian anti-free speech laws, and an immigrant birth rate that is often triple the indigenous birthrate, Western Europe finds herself in sorry condition.

There has, however, been a major surge in right-wing parties in countries like Belgium, Denmark, and Switzerland. The United Kingdom, which has long been without any substantial right-wing party, has seen the British National Party spreading across city councils in England and now poised to gain seats in the European union. Many in the Council of Conservative Citizens have followed the BNP closely over the years.

One party in Western Europe stands out above the rest. Vlaams Blok, meaning "Flemish Block" in Dutch, is by far the most successful Nationalist/Populist political party in Europe. They have become not only the political model, but also the inspiration and the hope of numerous other parties across Europe. Founded in 1977, this maverick party holds political rallies complete with folk dancers and medieval knights.

Vlaams Blok is a regional secessionist party for Flanders, the Dutch-speaking region of Belgium, which accounts for 60% of the Belgian population. Vlaams Blok wants Flanders to secede from Belgium. They want their "unique cultural identity" and language to be preserved. They also want to be the inspiration to Dutch speaking minorities in other European countries to preserve their identity. Vlaams Blok calls for the complete "reversal of erroneous multi-cultural policies." Vlaams Blok calls for the EU to have limited powers to interfere with state sovereignty and not to expand beyond the borders of Europe. Vlaams Blok believes in upholding the "traditional principles of European civilization." This includes freedom, law and order, solidarity of a common people, and the protection of the family.

Electoral Success in Flanders

In 2003, Vlaams Blok received over 24% of the vote for the Flemish Parliament, making it the largest single party in Flanders. In October of 2004, a Walloon court deemed Vlaams Blok to be a "racist" group, opening the entire membership to fines and criminal prosecutions. On November 9th, the Belgium Supreme Court upheld the ruling. Vlaams Blok was formally disbanded and re-organized as Vlaams Belang with a new platform. The platform could not contain language that could be construed by the left as "anti-immigrant," however it still calls for expatriation of immigrants "who reject, deny or fight against culture and European values like the separation of church and state, freedom of expression, and equality between men and women."

This absurdity of a "democratic" country banning one of its primary political parties is fueled by a desire of the pro-immigrant socialists to enforce its will on the rest of the population by any means necessary. Even though Vlaams Blok is already operating under a new name, they have lost most of their funding, [as a result of the court decision]. . . .

A Divided Country

In 1962, Belgium was formally divided. The French speaking part became Walloonia and the Dutch speaking part Flanders. All national parties split in half. Belgium is economically split as well—Walloonia is socialist with vast numbers of government employees while Flanders leans to a free-market economy. Flanders today has a significantly better economy, while Walloonia is a socialist basket-case subsidized on Flemish tax dollars.

Belgium has a bicameral parliament with parliamentary style elections. Any party that obtains at least 5% of the votes gets representation based on their percentage of the vote in both houses of Parliament. Belgium has a high voter turnout, over 90%, as voting is compulsory.

In 1977, a small Flemish nationalist party formed called Vlaams Blok. In 1991, Vlaams Blok gained seats in Parliament and continued to grow in every election. The "cordan sanitaire" was formed as an informal agreement between all the other parties to keep Vlaams Blok out of any coalitions. In the 1999 national elections, there were ten parties achieving 5% or more. Vlaams Blok received 9.65% of the vote, and became the fifth largest party. The Socialist ruling coalition was thrown into a panic and passed several extremely vague "Anti-Racism" laws designed to derail Vlaams Blok. The "Anti-Racism" laws make any member of a group found to be "racist" subject to fines and prosecution. It also puts the burden of proof on the accused, rather than the accuser. The socialist regime actually amended Belgium's constitution just to make the "Anti-Racism" law legal.

Party financing is entirely different than it is in America. Corporations are banned from donating money to a party. An individual can only donate a maximum of 125 Euros ($150 US). The majority of campaign financing comes from the state. Each party is given money based on their percentage of the vote received in the last election. Vlaams Blok received 325,000 Euros this year, representing most of its finances.

Immigrant violence, and the refusal of immigrants to accept European customs, is coming to a boiling point all across Europe.

If Vlaams Blok can be banned using the "Anti-Racism" laws, the socialists erase Vlaams Blok's finance for the next election (not to mention increasing the money their own parties will receive).

In 2000, elections for city councils and provincial councils were held and Vlaams Blok gained 15% of the overall vote. They achieved 33% of the vote in the city of Antwerp, Belgium's second largest city. Antwerp had long been Vlaams Blok's main stronghold.

Socialists Attack the "Nazis"

After the 2000 elections, the ruling socialists declared that Vlaams Blok was over represented because many of the country's half-million immigrants could not vote. In 2001, the Socialists passed legislation speeding up the process that would allow immigrants to vote. The Socialists believed, correctly, that new immigrants would vote socialist to expand their own welfare benefits.

In 2003, Vlaams Blok did even better in national elections, gaining 761,000 votes and 11.6% of the national vote. (The top vote getting party gained almost 1 million exactly.)

Next came the 2004 regional elections in Flanders. The socialist left launched a full scale war against Vlaams Blok declaring it a party of "beer swilling Skinheads," "fascists," and "nazis." When the votes were counted the nation was shocked. Vlaams Blok received 24.1% of the vote making it the single largest party in Flanders. In fact, Vlaams Blok received almost 250,000 more votes than it had in the previous national election. Had all the same people voted for Vlaams Blok in 2003, it would have been the largest party in Belgium. . . .

Then in June 2004, Vlaams Blok received over 14.3%, or 930,000 votes, in federal elections for the European Parliament giving them a chunk of Belgium's seats in the European Union.

In October of 2004, a socialist leaning court in Walloonia ruled that Vlaams Blok had indeed violated "Anti-Racism" laws and its membership was subject to prosecution unless it disbanded. The judge ruled that Vlaams Blok had an "intention to contribute to a campaign of hatred," because they published statistics of crime and welfare as well as the treatment of women by Muslims. Immediately after the ruling, numerous opinion polls showed that 45% of the citizens of Flanders wanted Vlaams Blok to be added to the ruling coalition in national and regional Parliaments.

On November 9th, the Belgian Supreme Court upheld the lower court's ruling. As noted above, Vlaams Blok immediately reorganized as Vlaams Belang. However, they will go into the next elections with very little money. . . .

Future Opportunities

Vlaams Belang received as much as 40% of the votes in the suburban areas around Antwerp. In fact, Vlaams Belang took 28.5% of the total votes in Antwerp Province making them the largest party in the province.

Overall, Vlaams Belang gained their biggest ground in rural areas, small villages, and suburbs with lots of white flight. A cartel of two center-right parties, also gained ground. The final results were 30.6% for a cartel of two center-right parties which have secessionist wings, 20.7% for Vlaams Belang,

19.6% for a cartel of two socialist parties, 18.9% for a cartel of two liberal parties, and 7.4% for an environmental party. That gives the center right and the far right a combined total of 51.3% dramatically shifting the balance of power and fore-telling a right-wing shake-up in the next Federal elections in 2007. . . .

Currently, the Belgium left is terrified as to what may happen in the 2007 election for Federal Parliament. Belgium's alliance of center-right parties may be large enough that they'll decide to break the "cordan sanitaire" and form a ruling coalition with Vlaams Belang instead of the socialist and liberal parties, thus shutting out the left wing from any important government positions.

Immigrant violence, and the refusal of immigrants to accept European customs, is coming to a boiling point all across Europe. Cities like Paris, Antwerp, Amsterdam, London and others all have areas that are "no-go" zones where white Europeans are attacked at random in their own homeland. Let us hope that Vlaams Blok, now Vlaams Belang, will continue to lead the way in promoting European identity and fighting the insanity of multiculturalism.

4

The Belgian Nationalist Party Promotes Extremism and Xenophobia

Angus Roxburgh

Angus Roxburgh is a foreign correspondent for the British Broadcasting Company. A journalist since 1984, he covered Eastern Europe during the Cold War and was once expelled from the Soviet Union.

The political party Vlaams Blok scapegoats immigrants and foreigners for the problems of Flanders, the Dutch-speaking region of Belgium. Their policies produce an atmosphere of intolerance and xenophobia. The party simply plays to the ignorance of the voters, using their fear of change to win votes without presenting workable policy ideas.

Like many of Europe's populist parties, the Vlaams Blok has exploited the changes that have taken place over recent decades in society: the emergence of multicultural communities, the dislocation caused by post-industrial economic change and the degeneration of mainstream coalitions that have ruled unchallenged for too long. As [Belgian political commentator] Swyngedouw concludes: 'The likely losers in this structural transformation are young, unskilled, blue-collar workers, lower-middle-class employees and small businessmen. These are the categories which have sought salvation in the Vlaams Blok, which has offered them the simple but misleading illu-

Angus Roxburgh, *Preachers of Hate: The Rise of the Far Right*. London: Gibson Square Books, 2005, pp. 191–96. Copyright © 2002 Angus Roxburgh. Reproduced by permission.

sion that once all the immigrants have gone, the prospects for welfare and the certainties of the past will all come flooding back.'

A Sour Atmosphere

Xenophobia has soured the atmosphere in the more national-istic Flemish districts of Belgium where substantial numbers of foreigners live—not just in places like Antwerp, but even in some areas near Brussels where the foreigners are largely other Europeans, associated with the European institutions. I happen to live in the suburb of Overijse, just outside Brussels proper, in Flanders. Registering to live there, as one is obliged to do, was a daunting experience, as all staff at the 'commune', or local council office, have been instructed to speak only Dutch—even to foreigners who have just arrived. When I approached the officials, with a smile and a 'Does anyone here speak English, please?' I was greeted with hostile stares from everyone in the room and a brisk shaking of heads. I had little option but to carry on in English, which, it emerged, the officials understood perfectly, but to which they replied only with nods and grimaces, and eventually a stab of the finger towards a notice which informed visitors that 'to preserve its cultural and linguistic identity Overijse is a Dutch-language-only commune', and that Dutch lessons were available at such-and-such an address. We struggled on, and my family was duly registered, but it was a frosty, unwelcoming event. It is the only place I have ever come across where people who speak English—the world's lingua franca—refuse to do so even to communicate with foreigners. Incidentally, this is purely state-sponsored xenophobia: it exists only within the local authority offices, whereas Flemish neighbours and shop-assistants in Overijse are happy to use English or French if a foreigner is struggling with Dutch. I can make no direct link to the Vlaams Blok—except that the commune does make itself available for its demonstrations—but this, it seemed to me, was a taste of what a Flanders run by the Blok would be like.

Target for Hate

Even worse are the leaflets and Vlaams Blok newspapers pushed through my letter-box. The February 2002 edition of *De 'Eigen Volk Eerst'-Krant* (Our Own Folk First-Newspaper) had the headline: 'Foreigners' right to vote—never!' For the first time it struck me that I, as much as any black African or Muslim, was a target for the Vlaams Blok's message of hate. The paper argued over several pages why foreigners should not be allowed to take part in Belgian elections. The most telling reason seemed to be that, in the Blok's view, most foreigners would vote for French-speaking candidates (and it was for this reason, it said, that the idea was allegedly supported only by Francophone Belgians).

> *[T]he Vlaams Blok thrives on public ignorance and prejudice.*

The newspaper featured an interview with a former Miss Belgium, Anke Van dermeersch, to lend glamour to the xenophobia. She began by explaining that she had nothing against foreigners, indeed, she was married to one . . . from Luxembourg. But she complained Belgium was now the easiest country in the world to settle in, thanks to the so-called *snel-belg-wet* ('fast-track citizenship law')—a one-off amnesty for illegal immigrants granted for a three-week period during October 2001, when aliens who had been in the country for at least six years were offered legal residence documents. The law, Ms Van dermeersch said, 'had allowed criminals from the east European mafia and Islamic terrorists to acquire Belgian identity cards.'

Fear of Islamicisation

Getting into her stride, she went on: 'It bothers me a lot that a number of things just can't be talked about any more in this country. Everyone knows that there are enormous problems with foreigners who get into crime. Everyone sees that the younger generation of foreigners sets itself against any form of authority (the police, etc.) and against our Western values. More and more often, our girls and women, when they're out in the street or in the trams, are insulted, or touched, or even assaulted. So I think the future is bleak. And the fact that more and more Muslim girls wear a headscarf is not hopeful for integration. As a woman I am concerned. . . . The Vlaams Blok has been saying for a year and a day that foreigners—not just north Africans but east Europeans too—are responsible for a large part of the crimes committed. . . . Hospitality is one thing, but we mustn't be crazy. There's been so much moaning recently about tolerance. I think we should say once and for all that that has to come from both sides. Because I don't want to go back to the Middle Ages. I don't want to have to go out in the street with a veil on tomorrow.' It sounded almost like incitement to white people to go out and rip the *hijab* (headscarf) from the heads of Muslim women.

The alleged imminent Islamicisation of Belgium is standard dogma in the Vlaams Blok. At a barbeque for party members in the small town of Torhout in August 2002, Dewinter was introduced by the chairman with the words: 'Here is Filip Dewinter, who will address you in one of Belgium's four national languages.' (This was a reference to a call by a radical Muslim leader in Antwerp—himself perhaps as extreme as Dewinter—for Arabic to be made an official language along with Dutch, French and German.) 'I predicted that this is how things would go!' Dewinter roared. 'It's because we never showed them our fist and put a stop to it.' He noted the 'segregation of swimming pools for men and women' for the sake of Muslims (in fact, this happens for only one hour per week, and was requested by a Catholic women's organisation as well as an Islamic group, for women who prefer to bathe alone), the alleged 'banning' of pork in state schools (simply not true, according to the city authorities), and a request for Arabic television to be subsidised by the government. 'Give them a finger and they will take an arm, and a whole body.' Dewinter was now pummelling the air with his fists, descending into sheer fantasy as his rabid rhetoric took over. 'That is why it is our historic task to stop the conquest by the hordes on Europe's borders, who want to put the crescent moon on our churches and city halls.'

Irresponsible Populism

Dewinter's style is almost a definition of populism. 'We just say what people think,' he told me. 'A lot of political issues and themes are taboo at the moment—it's impossible to speak about the immigrant problems, it's impossible to speak about the rise of crime. The politically correct parties don't want to speak about these things. We just say what people are thinking about this sort of issues, and that's the reason our party is doing very well. We are a non-conformist, non-traditional political party.' What is missing in such an approach is the sense of responsibility that a mainstream party exhibits—an awareness that a political party actually has to do more than simply parrot the uninformed ravings of the football stand. On the contrary, the Vlaams Blok thrives on public ignorance and prejudice. If telling the people that Flanders' Catholic churches are about to be turned into mosques wins votes, then it is worth saying.

5

Whites Feel Threatened By the Booming Hispanic Population

Roberto Lovato

Roberto Lovato is a Los Angeles-based writer with the Pacific News Service.

Large-scale immigration has pushed whites out of the majority in California and is shrinking their proportion of the population nationwide. This has caused a new sort of politics, white minority politics. This new politics makes itself felt in causes like anti-immigration activism and the formation of groups which combat "anti-white discrimination." The current governor of California, Arnold Schwartzenegger, has won votes by playing to whites who are angry about the demographic shifts in their state.

The enemy preaches "race hatred," according to *FrontPageMagazine*'s David Horowitz. It aims to undermine the very foundations of Anglo-American civilization—and perhaps, through sheer numbers and singleness of purpose, it will succeed. Horowitz was the featured speaker at a March rally held on the UCLA campus, where attendees denounced the "brain-washing," "evil propaganda" and "institutional racism" of their adversaries in a looming cultural war.

White Minority Politics

These white Republicans are all the forefront of a new wave of minority politics: white minority politics. Though rooted in California, this new politics of fear is cropping up across the country as its promoters redefine who is racial victim and who is racial oppressor, neatly inverting—and co-opting—the arguments and terms of the civil rights movement. . . .

Alamo-like fears of Latino takeover are emerging in jittery white enclaves across this national-security-driven country, in which one of every four Americans will be of Latino descent by 2050, according to a census report released this past March. Tom Tancredo, a Colorado Representative and chairman of the Congressional Immigration Reform Caucus, has since 9/11 regularly conflated Latino immigrants with "terrorist criminals" at meetings like one recently held in the predominantly white Los Angeles suburb La Canada. At that event, organizers displayed an unmanned aerial vehicle that they hope will track Latino immigrants at the border the way it tracks enemy combatants in Iraq. Tancredo also rails against Latinos who threaten "our civilization" with textbooks that describe "defenders of the Alamo as slave owners, land speculators, and Indian killers."

Barbarians from the South

The Sierra Club recently fended off a hostile takeover by a new breed of well-heeled, anti-immigrant, anti-Latino activists who believe they're defending American civilization against the balkanizing and breeding barbarians from the South. Mediagenic scholars like commentator and bestselling *Mexifornia* author Victor Davis Hanson provide intellectual cover for this hate-based movement with frequent appearances on television, radio and lecture circuits and on the Internet. (Hanson's work is supported by the Claremont and Hoover institutes, both of which receive significant funding from the Olin Foundation, which has also supported notorious *Bell Curve* author Charles Murray and the war think tank Project for the New American Century, or PNAC.) Cable TV ranters Bill O'Reilly, Lou Dobbs and Sean Hannity have added their voices to the chorus warning against the Latino menace. Most recently, national security guru Samuel Huntington called US Latinos "the single most immediate and most serious challenge to America's traditional identity" in his new book, *Who Are We? The Challenges to America's National Identity*. What Huntington calls "The Hispanic Challenge" is portrayed as the cause of a "clash of civilizations" in the homeland.

Whites, who are still more than 70 percent of California's electorate, are just 47 percent of the population and will be outnumbered by Latinos within twenty years.

Orange County is the epicenter of one of the most dramatic demographic and political shifts of the developed world. These changes are spinning identities and political processes with the speed and relentlessness of Disneyland's whirling Mad Hatter teacup ride, which made me dizzy in the late 1960s, when I was a minority (80 percent of the population identified itself as "white") among the mostly white workers and white Mouseketeers near the Davy Crockett canoes in Frontierland and the boats cruising the exotic tropical jungles in Adventureland.

Demographic Shift

Since then, as many as 2 million mostly white Californians have fled to what may have appeared to be less exotic places, like Florida, Alaska and Texas. During the 1990s California gained more than 4 million residents, mostly newborns and immigrant Latinos. As a result, whites, who are still more than 70 percent of California's electorate, are just 47 percent of the population and will be outnumbered by Latinos within twenty years. Rich and poor white voters holding down the racial ramparts in the state are being ideologically re-equipped as foot soldiers in the next phase of the conservative suburban political revolution that gave California—and eventually the country—its first actor-politico, the late Ronald Reagan, who stoked the members of white voter fear while pounding the drum of national security. Unlike the more naked racial sign-posts and rituals of the Reagan era (signs in parks that said NO DOGS, NO NEGROES, NO MEXICANS; snarling dogs that kept nonwhite students at bay), today's signs are more coded (NO FUTBOL, NO STREET VENDING, etc.). But the more subtle messages are more widely and effectively distributed by think tanks, academies, radio pundits and right-wing politicians, who have created an industry that interprets whiteness in an unprecedented context—in which many whites feel uncomfortably surrounded by "minorities." In this spirit, for example, Arnold Schwarzenegger made hay out of driver's license wielding immigrants and Indian gaming authorities in the recall election last year. . . .

Organizing to Combat Racism Against Whites

The Schwarzenegger message played especially well with older white voters. An especially angry member of that aging vanguard is Lou Calabro, head of the European American Issues Forum (EAIF), which he co-founded following a pro—Proposition 209 rally in 1996. After telling me that the magazines I write for, including *The Nation*, are "egg-sucking, left-wing liberal extremists with an agenda of their own," the energetic, stalky, blue-eyed, 70-year-old former police lieutenant arranged to meet me at his favorite grill around the corner from the San Francisco police station where EAIF, which he says has 300 members, holds its meetings. Chinese residents are becoming the majority population in the neighborhood where we chatted over steak and potatoes. Calabro tells me that EAIF's primary mission is to "minimize discrimination and defamation against whites." To pursue this mission, EAIF works to raise awareness of hate crimes against whites ("Did you know that 90 percent of interracial hate crimes between blacks and whites are perpetrated by blacks—against whites?")

and to address discrimination against whites before city councils, health bureaucracies and, especially, schools.

Calabro and EAIF are hard to situate politically; they have not been labeled "hate groups" by organizations like the Southern Poverty Law Center. They *have* met with mayors, state legislators,city council members and other establishment figures in Northern California, and they draw on the reports and messages generated by think tank fellows like Hanson. Calabro is quick to distance his organization from white fringe groups, which, he says, promote hatred as much as black, Latino and Jewish groups do.

White Student Organizations

The EAIF was involved in the controversial case of 15-year-old Lisa McClelland, who petitioned authorities at Freedom High School to form a Caucasian Club in predominantly (64 percent) white Oakley in Contra Costa County, just an hour's drive from liberal San Francisco. School authorities expressed grave concerns about her petition, but never denied the request to form the club. Still, McClelland and Calabro, her "informal adviser," have filed a complaint with the US Department of Education's Office of Civil Rights for denying Lisa liberty at Freedom High. Since then, several other California schools have started white student organizations, including the Caucasian Student Union at Piedmont High School and "European Ancestry" club at San Jose's Independence High.

Calabro shared with me an EAIF kit, which contained instructions on "Forming Campus Chapters" at high schools and colleges ("Example: In a speech class, speak about EAIF recognition and note any positive reaction"): a copy of California Assembly Resolution 91, designating October "European American Heritage Month" in California; and a *Wall Street Journal* op-ed by classics and history professor—and PNAC supporter—Donald Kagan With a background picture of a breastplated Augustus Caesar pointing to the future of

Pax Romana and, implicitly, its modern imitators. Kagan's article, "Why History Matters," contrasts the virtues of freedom and classics against the vices of civilizational decline.

6

Hardcore Racists Exploit Concern Over Immigration to Gain Recruits

Chip Berlet

Chip Berlet is an analyst at Political Research Associates who specializes in extremist movements. He is the author of Right-wing Populism in America: Too Close for Comfort.

Concerns over immigration enable white supremacist groups to expand beyond their normally small circle of potential recruits. Neo-Nazi groups have become sophisticated, using music and media to promote a racially based anti-immigrant message. By distributing the literature of mainstream anti-immigration groups, the supremacist groups conceal their radical aims.

American white supremacist groups have a long and ugly history of using anxieties over immigration as a recruitment tool. It's happening again—with a vengeance. As nativist [anti-immigrant] sentiments have hardened and spread, white-supremacist and neo-Nazi groups have stepped up their recruitment efforts—and it's working. The Southern Poverty Law Center (SPLC) has documented a sharp rise in the number of such groups nationally, and Mark Potok, editor of the SPLC's *Intelligence Report*, says the growth is directly related to these groups' new emphasis on immigration. "The furor over immigration policies is a critical factor in the 33 percent increase in hate groups between 2000 and 2005," says Potok, and

Chip Berlet, "The Hard Edge of Hatred," *Nation Online*, August 15, 2006. www.the nation.com. Reproduced by permission.

"this growth is fed by publicity stunts, belligerent attitudes and actions, and piggybacking on public fears about immigrants."

For example, on May 6, the National Knights of the Ku Klux Klan [KKK] held an anti-immigration rally in Russellville, Alabama, that drew some 300 supporters, including some hard-core neo-Nazis. Robed Klansmen lit a 22-foot-high cross, the SPLC reported, and yelled, "Let's get rid of the Mexicans!" White-supremacist and neo-Nazi groups are also aggressively leafleting neighborhoods in the American heartland, hunting for recruits at rallies staged by more mainstream anti-immigration groups, and holding anti-immigration rallies of their own.

Racial Nationalism

The synergy between mainstream anti-immigration groups and hardcore white supremacists is founded on a common belief in a form of racial nationalism (unconscious, in the case of some mainstreamers) that assumes European settlers comprise a "native-born" population that constitutes the "real" America. Organized white supremacist groups, however, talk about the survival of the white race in explicit terms.

Neo-Nazis, for example, add an obsession with the myth of an "Aryan Race." They see immigrants of color not just destroying American culture, as the mainstreamers do, but also openly describe dark-skinned immigrants as racially inferior and a form of biological pollution or disease that needs to be expelled or eradicated. "If you tolerate multiracialism," warns National Vanguard leader Kevin Alfred Strom, "then your children will suffer and die."

One catchy song they sing is called 'Aryan Man Awake.'

Like others on the hard edge of the new nativism, Strom is highly critical of mainstream anti-immigration types who, he believes, know that "Mexican immigration threatens the survival of the White race and White civilization," but who hide behind cowardly platitudes like "overcrowding," "assimilation," and "the failure of new immigrants to learn English." Strom's National Vanguard, along with the National Socialist Movement, Volksfront, and similar neo-Nazi groups, has eclipsed the KKK in the role of preserving the bloodline of the "white race" in the United States.

The new neo-Nazi movement even has networking groups such as Stormfront.org, a site which promotes activism and cooperation among members of a variety of neo-Nazi groups as well as white supremacists not affiliated with a specific organization.

Music and Posters

The poster sisters for the anti-immigrant Aryan revival are blonde and blue-eyed Lynx and Lamb Gaede, fraternal twins who perform at white-supremacist rallies as the musical group Prussian Blue. At age 11 they rallied in matching "Stop Immigration" T-shirts. Now, at 14, they are the little darlings of the neo-Nazi anti-immigrant *Kulturkampf.* They told an interviewer for *Vice Magazine* that the most important social issue facing the white race was "[n]ot having enough white babies born to replace ourselves and generally not having good-quality white people being born." One catchy song they sing is called "Aryan Man Awake."

The Prussian Blue Internet home page links to the National Vanguard website. That website carries several well-designed anti-immigrant flyers that supporters can download, reproduce on home printers or at local copy shops, and distribute. The flyers from National Vanguard and a similar group from which they split, National Alliance, are far more visually striking and well-written than most grassroots neo-Nazi literature, and at first glance appear to have no connection to a white supremacist group. In Arizona this July, "JennyP" told her allies on the National Vanguard networking forum hosted by the Stormfront website that their unit had just finished distributing 16,000 of these flyers.

According to an Arizona National Vanguard leader, "approximately 100,000 have been distributed in the past two years in Arizona," mostly in the Phoenix area. "Not everybody who is receptive contacts us," he says. "Some people will just start visiting our website and listening to our radio broadcasts," he says. "Some will become active supporters of our cause; others will become passive supporters." Anti-immigrant flyers from National Vanguard also have been reported in California, Florida, Massachusetts, Nevada, New Mexico, and North Carolina; anti-racist activists suspect flyers are appearing in dozens of states.

More KKK chapters have started appearing in the past few years . . . and many of them are highlighting immigration as an issue.

Hiding Behind Mainstream Groups

Stormfront also hosts discussions on how white supremacists can hand out flyers from more mainstream anti-immigrant groups such as Americans for Legal Immigration Political Action Committee (ALIPAC). Participants said they had already downloaded and distributed the ALIPAC literature: "Nice Flyer," commented "Iceman88," "I bet you'd have zero complaints from the cops or news media." "Exactly," responded "Kenny," "there's no sign of what the jew media would call 'racist.'"

National Vanguard and National Alliance are not the only neo-Nazis who have learned to tone down their public rhetoric to seek recruits from a broader base and appear more "mainstream." Sounding uncannily like a blue-collar populist politician from the first half of the 20th century, the leader of the National Socialist Movement [NSM] told an Indiana audience in 2003 that immigrants were "dragging down the economy and stealing jobs . . . making a lot of Americans feel like second class citizens."

NSM may now be the largest neo-Nazi group in the US with over 50 units in some 30 states. Founded in 1974, NSM has a paramilitary structure and conducts armed training sessions for whites, according to the Anti-Defamation League. NSM already had a mission that fit the new nativist outbreak: It is "dedicated to the preservation of our Proud Aryan Heritage."

More KKK chapters have started appearing in the past few years, reports Potok, and many of them are highlighting immigration as an issue. Devin Burghart at the Center for New Community, another watchdog group, points out that the contemporary idea for a vigilante-style anti-immigrant "border patrol" was first hatched in the 1970s by KKK leaders. Now this tactic appears to have broader appeal. Chris Simcox ran a vigilante-style militia, then reinvented the group as the Minuteman Civil Defense Corps (MCDC), softening the image and the rhetoric in the process. When neo-Nazis said they would help recruit for the MCDC, Simcox publicly declared they were unwelcome.

Violent Rhetoric in Mainstream Channels

At the same time, some neo-Nazi groups are toning down their rhetoric to capitalize on mainstream anti-immigration sentiments in Middle America. Others are sending their violent rhetoric through mainstream channels.

Last March, SPLC reported that New Jersey radio host Hal Turner was challenging neo-Nazis to up the ante: "I advocate using extreme violence against illegal aliens. Clean your guns. Have plenty of ammunition. Find out where the largest gathering of illegal aliens will be near you. . . . [T]hen do what has to be done. . . . All of you who think there's a peaceful solution to these invaders are wrong. We're going to have to start killing these people." One neo-Nazi who agreed posted this on a web forum: "The bad news is many whites will die [but it] will be grand [and if] you have a good defense line and lots of ammo the carnage will be orgasmic."

7

Whites Should Work Together to Advance Their Interests

Jamie Glazov and Jared Taylor

Jamie Glazov is the managing editor at FrontPageMagazine.com online magazine which hosted a symposium on white nationalism. One of the participants was Jared Taylor. Taylor is the editor of the white nationalist publication, American Rennaisance.

Historically, the United States has been white supremacist, with even enlightened politicians such as Abraham Lincoln promoting separation, or, failing that, a heirachy of races with whites on top. Racially conscious whites today do not want supremacy, but do believe that when left to their own devices, people will segregate into racial groups. Racial identity politics is a natural phenomenon. The current system in which whites who are racially conscious are accused of racism while other races are free to advance their interests is a mistake, something more and more people understand.

[Glazov:] *(1) How does white nationalism differ from old style white supremacy?*
[Taylor:] Abraham Lincoln stated the classic case for white supremacy in his September 1858 debate with Stephen Douglas:

> [T]here is a physical difference between the white and black races which I believe will ever forbid the two races living together on terms of social and political equality. And in as

Jamie Glazov, "White Nationalism: A Symposium," *FrontPageMagazine.com*, January 10, 2003. www.frontpagemag.com. Reproduced by permission.

much as they cannot so live, while they do remain together, there must be a position of superior and inferior, and I as much as any other man am in favor of having the superior position assigned to the white race.

It is worth noting, however, that white supremacy was, for Lincoln, only a second-best solution. He understood very well that a legally hierarchical society that characterized one group as superior to the other was unjust. Hierarchy was nevertheless preferable to any attempt at political and social equality which, he believed, would be disastrous for whites.

Please note the phrase "while they do remain together" in the above quotation. Like many prominent Americans, he thought the only fair, long-term solution to the race problem was "colonization," or voluntary expatriation of blacks. "The enterprise is a difficult one," he wrote in 1857, "but 'when there is a will there is a way;' and what colonization needs most is a hearty will." Thomas Jefferson was a strong proponent of colonization, as were James Monroe, Andrew Jackson, Daniel Webster, Stephen Douglas, William Seward, Francis Scott Key, Gen. Winfield Scott, and two Chief Justices of the Supreme Court, John Marshall and Roger Taney.

The basis for the early-American desire for separation (or hierarchy if separation was not possible) was the conviction that race is a significant part of individual and collective identity, that multi-racial societies are inherently unstable, and that whites and blacks therefore cannot live together without friction from which whites will suffer more greatly than blacks. These convictions are shared by all racially conscious whites today, and in this respect their thinking is identical to that of what the question describes as "old-style white supremacy."

Today's racially-conscious whites agree that separation is the only fair, long-term solution. Nevertheless, they part company with Lincoln in rejecting hierarchical race relations. In the past, whites have tried to square the circle by means of

Jim Crow, segregation, apartheid, and pass laws but the inherent tensions of multi-racialism are simply too great to be contained.

A level of racial separation sufficient for most purposes could be achieved simply by recognizing rather than denying the obvious: that a preference for people of one's own group is natural, normal, and healthy. From this would follow the abolition of all anti-discrimination laws, the reestablishment of neighborhood schools, and a thorough overhaul of immigration, which only increases racial diversity and the potential for conflict. . . .

More and more whites now recognize that is was only they who have shed their racial consciousness, while every other racial group unabashedly advances its collective interests at the expense of whites.

This is why immigration is so important. Our color-blind immigration policy is based on the assumption that race is an illegitimate criterion for defining "living space" or any other space. But if race is a legitimate criterion, why should whites (or blacks) welcome the arrival of Asians and Hispanics, who are alien to us both? In any case, our polychrome but overwhelmingly non-white immigration stream is only creating infinite varieties of racial conflict to overlie and complicate the original black/white divide. Racial diversity is a terrible source of conflict and tension; it is not a strength. . . .

(2) Given our national emphasis on multiculturalism and identity politics, isn't it reasonable for white Americans to want to join the celebration of group pride and group self-determination?

Identity politics have not arisen because of some kind of "national emphasis." They reflect the tribal nature of man. Until only a few decades ago, whites practised identity politics of the kind common among non-whites, and this was reflected in segregation, anti-miscegenation laws, and an immigration policy designed to keep the country majority-white. What we call the "civil rights movement" was a historically unprecedented attempt to dismantle racial consciousness for all Americans in the hope of building a society in which race did not matter.

That is what whites, at any rate, thought was the ultimate goal of the movement, and many tried very hard to rid themselves of any sentiment of racial solidarity. They passed laws outlawing freedom of association based on race, they forcibly integrated schools, they opened the country to millions of non-white immigrants, and even instituted officially-sanctioned policies of racial discrimination against themselves under the euphemistic name of "affirmative action." All this was an astonishing betrayal of their own interests, but whites tried to persuade themselves that losing their institutions, watching their neighborhood and schools deteriorate, and condemning their grandchildren to minority status was somehow ennobling.

More and more whites now recognize that it was only they who have shed their racial consciousness, while every other racial group unabashedly advances its collective interests at the expense of whites. Whites have practised unilateral disarmament and are discovering the consequences. More and more whites understand this, but many still "celebrate diversity," even though to do so is to celebrate their own declining numbers and influence.

(3) Do white nationalist leaders champion some legitimate grievances that are not being addressed satisfactorily by mainstream political leaders?

Let us not overlook some very important facts:

Only whites outside the "mainstream" are prepared to point out the obvious: there is a great deal of black-on-white violent crime and very little white-on-black crime.

"Affirmative action" is nothing more than officially sanctioned racial discrimination against whites.

"Affirmative action" for immigrants is an outrage that would be unthinkable if whites had even the faintest sense of racial solidarity.

Massive third-world immigration is transforming this country in countless undesirable ways.

It is an obvious double standard to encourage every non-white group to celebrate their heritage and achievements while condemning similar expressions by whites as "racism."

Black and Hispanic failure is due largely to differences in ability rather than to "oppression" by whites.

Blaming the failures of non-whites on white "racism" only encourages non-whites to hate whites. . . .

(4) What do you see as the future of American race relations? Will we come together as a nation or become increasingly divided over issues of race?

For decades, the Communists tried to build a society in which selfishness could be abolished, in which all would live "from each according to his ability to each according to his need." This attempt ended in tyrannical failure because Communism was a misreading of human nature. The goal of multi-racialism and the doctrine that diversity is a strength are likewise misreadings of human nature. All around the world, diversity—be it of race, religion, language, tribe, or culture—is at the heart of every sustained blood-letting.

Race is a biological fact. It is the most prominent and intractable fault line in any society. The idea that racial diversity can work in America even though it has never worked anywhere ever is to assume that the United States has abolished the laws of human nature. To the extent that multi-racialism has worked here at all, it is due to the willingness of whites to sacrifice their own interests in order to build a country in which race is supposed to dwindle into insignificance.

Non-whites don't even pretend they want to build such a society. They quite naturally want America to reflect their cultures, celebrate their heroes and holidays, and not those of whites. As whites begin to understand the dangers of the forces they have set in motion, more and more will brave the insults and begin to work for their entirely legitimate interests as a race.

8

The New White Supremacists Mask Racism with Pseudo-Intellectualism

Dennis Roddy

Dennis Roddy is a columnist for the Pittsburgh Post-Gazette.

Jared Taylor exemplifies the latest tactics of the white supremacy movement. While Taylor trills himself as a race-relations expert, the organizations he is associated with promote racism. Taylor uses his impressive résumé to get access to mainstream media that are unaware of his real opinions. He then promotes white supremacist ideas using dubious science and smooth arguments.

On Martin Luther King Jr. Day last week, when much of the nation took a holiday, "race-relations expert" Jared Taylor was hard at work. He began at 6:45 A.M. with an interview with a Columbus radio station. At 7:05 he was on the air in Orlando. An hour later his voice greeted morning commuters in Huntington, W.Va.

At 10:10 A.M., he was introduced no fewer than four times as "race relations expert Jared Taylor" on Fred Honsberger's call-in show on the Pittsburgh Cable News Channel. Four hours later, he was back on the air with Honsberger on KDKA radio, where he repeated the message he'd been thumping all day: Martin Luther King Jr. was a philanderer, a plagiarist and a drinker who left a legacy of division and resentment, and was unworthy of a national holiday.

Not What He Seems

What Taylor did not say, and what Honsberger didn't seem to know until I picked up the phone and called in myself, was that Jared Taylor believes black people are genetically predisposed to lower IQs than whites, [and] are sexually promiscuous because of hyperactive sex drives. Race-relations expert Jared Taylor keeps company with a collection of racists, racial "separatists" and far-right extremists.

Taylor heads the Virginia-based New Century Foundation. Its board of directors has included a leader of the Council of Conservative Citizens, successor to the White Citizens Councils of the 1960s. A former board member represented the American Friends of the British National Party, a neo-fascist and anti-Semitic far-right group in England. Another board member is an anti-immigration author who has also reviewed books for a Holocaust denial journal.

Race-relations expert Jared Taylor publishes *American Renaissance* magazine, which features an array of pseudoscientific studies that purport to show the folly of multiculturalism and the inherent failure of the races to live together. Or, as Taylor once wrote, "If whites permit themselves to be displaced, it is not just the high culture of the West that could disappear but such things as representative government, rule of law and freedom of speech, which whites usually get right and everyone else usually gets wrong."

Maybe Taylor doesn't know any Klansmen, but before selling his house he might have to spray for them.

What Taylor represents and how he got himself on no fewer than a half-dozen radio and television stations in large markets to denounce Martin Luther King illustrates the new tactics of white supremacy. Employing the dispassionate language of sociological and genetic studies, and under the veneer of academic inquiry, an assortment of highly educated people now push the theory that everything from unwed motherhood in Atlanta to economic collapse in Gambia can be explained by the genetic code imprinted on the races.

Providing Intellectual Heft

With a magazine that sounds as if it might be found on a coffee table in Mt. Lebanon, a degree from Yale, and fluency in three languages, Taylor easily found takers when his assistants blasted e-mails to scores of radio stations offering a Martin Luther King Day guest.

"Not everyone celebrates the legacy of Martin Luther King," the pitch reads. "Editor of *American Renaissance* magazine and race-relations expert Jared Taylor would be pleased to offer your listeners a view of Dr. King that challenges conventional wisdom."

Taylor's résumé, conveniently linked to the e-mail, was formidable: bachelor's from Yale, master's in economics from the Institute for Political Study in Paris, business consultant in Japan, author of a quartet of books, two of them on race. It was all true, but gave nary a hint of what Taylor is really about.

"Jared Taylor is the cultivated, cosmopolitan face of white supremacy," said Mark Potok, editor of *Intelligence Report*, the magazine of the Southern Poverty Law Center. "He is the guy who is providing the intellectual heft, in effect, to modern-day Klansmen."

Taylor insists leftists are simply using that language to demonize intellectuals who take on sensitive issues.

"I've never been a member of the Klan. I've never known a person who is a member of the Klan," Taylor told Honsberger.

It's hard to say if Taylor knows any Klansmen, but they certainly know him. When conservative author Dinesh D'Souza attended one of Taylor's *American Renaissance* conferences, he bumped into David Duke, former Klansman and segregationist, chatting with Taylor. Another Klan stalwart is

Don Black, whose neo-Nazi Web site, Stormfront.org, is a clearinghouse for extremist literature. Black gained celebrity in 1981 when he was arrested as he boarded a boat for Dominica where he and nine other mercenaries planned to overthrow that predominantly black island's government and install a white colonial junta. Potok, whose group occasional infiltrates Taylor's gatherings, sent me a photo of Black sitting at Jared Taylor's kitchen table, a beer in hand.

Maybe Taylor doesn't know any Klansmen, but before selling his house he might have to spray for them.

Taylor's strategy when I confronted him was to deny things that are easily proven. He insisted *American Renaissance* had never published an article in which theocratic writer Rousas J. Rushdoony denounced interracial marriage as Biblically unsound.

Against Interracial Marriage

I refer Taylor to the July 2001 edition of his own magazine, in which H. A. Scott Trask calls intermarriage "racial suicide" and observes: "The Late Rousas J. Rushdoony points out that Biblical law and example is against all kinds of unequal yoking. The burden of the law is thus against inter-religious, interracial, and inter-cultural marriages, in that they normally go against the very community which marriage is designed to establish."

One of the more tendentious exchanges took place when I challenged Taylor to state whether he had published articles in "the quarterly of the British National Party."

"I don't believe the BNP has a quarterly," Taylor replied.

He's right. They have a monthly. It's called "Spearhead," and it carried Taylor's writings in the early 1990s, under his other name, Samuel Taylor. This relationship is no accident. Taylor's conferences have included speeches on white nationalism by none other than Nick Griffin, a Holocaust denier and leader of the BNP. Spearhead's editor, John Tyndall, toured the

United States last year. After stops to visit David Duke in New Orleans, where Tyndall noted with disapproval the large number of racial minorities, he moved on to Oakton, Va., where he stayed at Taylor's home.

Before that, Tyndall was treated to lunch by Samuel Francis, one of the board members of Taylor's New Century Foundation.

A decade ago, Francis was fired by *The Washington Times* for a racist speech he delivered at an American Renaissance Conference. Since then he has busied himself as editor of *The Citizens Informer*, monthly paper of The Council of Conservative Citizens. The paper features regular accounts of invasions by non-white immigrants, black-on-white crime and the need for racial purity.

Those who would suggest that the Council's connections to Francis and Francis's ties to Taylor are guilt-by-association might want to consider the New Century Foundation's own tax filings for 1999. On line 80 of their IRS Form 990, Taylor's foundation lists the Council of Conservative Citizens as an organization to which it is "related . . . through common membership, governing bodies, trustees, officers, etc."

May Deny It, but His Friends and Associates Are Racists

This was the very year that the Council of Conservative Citizens included a link on its Web site to the Free Market Party. The link was quickly cancelled when the Free Market Party's founder and sole member, Richard Baumhammers, left his Mt. Lebanon home with a pistol in hand, killed his Jewish neighbor, set her house afire, then embarked on a two-county rampage that targeted Asians, Indians and blacks. In all, five people died. Baumhammers was concerned, like those who circle Jared Taylor's planet of intellect, about the expansion of non-white races.

None of this, of course, would meet with the approval of Jared Taylor, race-relations expert, who took the pains to tell Honsberger that people should be free to marry whomever they want, and that suggestions he is a racist are meant simply to shut up anyone who wants to rationally discuss race outside the norms of safe politics.

Such assurances would be more comforting if the audience that orbits planet Jared did not include members of the National Alliance, the Council of Conservative Citizens, the British National Party, Don Black, and David Duke. Taylor says he doesn't know any Klansmen. What is scarier is that he doesn't know his audience—and the radio stations that gave him a platform on Martin Luther King Jr. Day didn't really know their guest.

9

Women Play a Subordinate but Vital Role in White Supremacist Groups

Kathleen M. Blee

Kathleen M. Blee is Professor of Sociology at the University of Pittsburgh; she researches gender and racism.

In recent years, white supremacist groups have put increasing emphasis on recruiting women. Women's roles differ in the various white supremacist groups. Traditional organizations such as the Ku Klux Klan promote women as caretakers of the family. Neo-Nazi groups permit more scope for direct activism by females. White supremacist groups hold the childbearing role of women in high regard, but in reality racist women are reluctant to have large families.

Women hold a perplexing role in modern organized racism. Historically, racist groups in the United States, with only sporadic exceptions, have been the province of white men. This is not surprising, given the deep misogyny and exultation of white-male privilege that underlies much racist rhetoric. Yet in recent years, organized racist groups in the United States have increasingly recruited white Aryan women as members. It is difficult to ascertain the exact membership of the racist movement, but it is likely that women are between 25 and 50 percent of the new recruits in a number of

Kathleen M. Blee, "Women and Organized Racism," *Home-Grown Hate: Gender and Organized Racism.* Danvers, MA: Routledge, 2004, pp. 49–61. Copyright © 2004 by Routledge. Republished with permission of Routledge, conveyed through Copyright Clearance Center, Inc.

prominent racist groups. Women are sought as members to bolster the size of floundering racist groups. A number of male racist leaders also regard women as safer recruits than men, less likely to commit nonracist crimes or to have past criminal records that would draw them and the group to the attention of the police.

Familial Roles

Women's activities in organized racism differ considerably across groups. In general, Christian Identity and Klan groups tend to emphasize women's familial and social roles, while women in some white-power skinhead and other neo-Nazi groups are involved in more direct action, playing what I term "operative" roles. But these distinctions are often blurred. Groups overlap in their memberships, and women move between groups. Even groups that share a similar racist philosophy vary in their treatment of women members, reflecting their different histories, their leaders' ideas, and their balance of male and female members. In general, the roles of racist women fall into three categories: familiar, social, and operative.

The most common activities for women in organized racism are racial elaborations of the domestic roles to which women are traditionally assigned. Racist activist women are expected to assume tasks associated with creating and nurturing a racist family. Because some segments of organized racism, especially Ku Klux Klan groups, emphasize that organized racism is "like a family," the scope of those tasks is not clear. Sometimes the racist family is invoked to refer to women's responsibilities to their husbands and children. At other times, it denotes women's obligation to sustain a collective "family" of organized racists. Many racist leaders try to create a familial atmosphere by stitching together political and recreational activities that promote loyalty and commitment from their followers. As Robert Miles of Aryan Nations told one reporter:

"No one who joins these circles is ever without family. Each of us is the father and the mother, the brother and the sister of every white child who's within our ranks."

[W]omen racists are told to fulfill their obligations to male intimates and to the racist movement by bearing Aryan babies.

Purpose and Commitment

Nearly every Klanswoman I interviewed framed her discussion of organized racism partly in terms of family, claiming that organized racism promoted "family-like" qualities of caring and mutual responsibility among its members. Although, as I show later, many Klanswomen have specific criticisms of their groups, on an abstract level they insist that the Klan's ideal follows a family model. "Everyone's real supportive and, naturally you're going to have your little arguments here and there, but . . . basically, they're all real supportive, just like a big family," concluded a Klanswoman. An Aryan supremacist claimed that her racist colleagues were "part of my life, like family." A Nazi said that the thing she liked best in the group was "the camaraderie and the sense we get of having an extended family. The kinship we feel is probably the most important thing to all involved." Another claimed that "the unity between people who live so far apart is amazing. It is its own family." A Southern woman made a Klan rally sound like a family reunion: "We'd all be together. The guys would play football. And it was like a big family, togetherness. It was the perfect utopia." Just as threats and conspiracies are understood by racist women largely in terms of their impact on immediate family and on daily life, so too the "virtue" of being in a racist group is often expressed in terms of its impact on self and family. A member of a violent Aryan group summarized how she felt about the group by saying: "It's given me more purpose and commitment in my life and I think it's helped me get closer to . . . my family, my friends. It's strengthened bonds of commitment."

Making Babies

In most racist groups, women are expected to mother their immediate families as well as the larger racist "family." Except in a few racist skinhead and neo-Nazi groups, women racists are told to fulfill their obligations to male intimates and to the racist movement by bearing Aryan babies. Cautioning racist men that "selecting a proper mate is the only way to give us the possibility in life to improve the heritary [*sic*] makeup of the coming generation," racist groups make it clear that racial obligation includes racial procreation. Such pronouncements are particularly frequent in Christian Identity and neo-Nazi groups that emphasize long-term planning for a racist future. This maternal responsibility is made explicit in the recruiting efforts of some groups that seek to win the "birth-rate war" by enlisting race-conscious white Aryan women who will give birth to a large number of children.

In reality, the childbearing patterns and expectations of racist activist women are more mixed than the glorification of fertility in racist propaganda might suggest. On the one hand, several women I interviewed spoke with enthusiasm about their potential or actual contributions to increasing the white population, including one neo-Nazi who described being in a racist recruitment video "pregnant and strolling down the street with my baby and [being] so proud." Similarly, a skin-girl interviewed by sociologist Mark Hamm commented that "what people don't know is that the [skinhead group] are strong into family values and strong anti-drug. There are eleven women in our group and eight are pregnant. This is the most important way we can carry, on with the white power tradition." An eighteen-year-old woman interviewed by a re-porter at an Aryan Fest prided herself on supporting the white movement even before she had her own babies by contributing toward movement drives for "cribs, baby clothes, [and] diapers" for "white families starting out."

Reality is Mixed

On the other hand, many women in my study who were childless at the time of their interview expressed a desire to have no more than three or four children. Although a few predicted vaguely that they would have "a big white family" or that they wanted "as many [children] as possible," most were like a neo-Nazi who alluded to pressure in the movement to have many babies, commenting that she would have "of course more than the typical one or two that the women of today want" but insisting that she was "not really aiming for ten either." A skinhead said that she supported the idea of having a lot of children—"at least four"—but that she was not willing to begin having babies until she and her boyfriend were financially and geographically stable and "prepared to raise her children in a decent environment." Another, an aspiring racist, told a reporter that the emphasis on babies—the insistence of male skinhead leaders that "the purpose of intercourse is to have as many white Christian babies as possible"—made her and her girlfriends reluctant to pursue their involvement in the racist movement.

Women with children and those older than thirty tended to be the most conservative in their childbearing goals. Most claimed that they did not want any additional children beyond the one or two they already had. One Klanswoman lowered her voice as she confided: "My husband wanted seven kids. I had two. I don't want any more." A skinhead, pregnant with her first child, concluded that she would have "only as many [children] as we can afford. I wouldn't want to deprive children of what they need just to have more." Some women even elaborated medical steps they had taken to ensure that they would not again become pregnant.

Teaching Hatred

Racist women are also held responsible for socializing their children into racial and religious bigotry. They often provide verbal instruction in the norms of racist living, such as direct admonitions "to stay away from nigger children." Sometimes their cautions are more indirect. For example, a skinhead mother recounted a conversation she had had with her elementary-school-aged daughter, a story oddly preceded by the mother's assurance that "I don't push her to believe any beliefs." "My daughter understands," the mother insisted. "She knows she's a special person. . . . It's the little things, [like] when she didn't know what a black kid was, I explained that she's different because of color, to let her know that she shouldn't be involved with nonwhite."

The children are ushered into a world of racial and religious hatred at a very early age. Homes are strewn with drawings, photos, flyers, videos, and pamphlets filled with vicious lies and threats against racial and religious enemies. In one house, a child's high chair featured a hand-scrawled swastika on the back. In another, children's crayons lay on flyers denouncing Jews as inhuman. Still others displayed pictures of lynchings on living-room walls or newspaper clippings about the bombing of the Oklahoma City federal building on refrigerator doors. Male leaders of racist groups, too, are involved in efforts to socialize youths as racist activists. A particularly pernicious means of targeting the very young is the racist comic book, such as the *New World Order Comix* published by the National Alliance and distributed by skinhead groups.

Social Roles

Women must also act as the social facilitators of racist groups, an expectation nearly as deep-seated as that making them responsible for bearing white children and raising them as racists. The importance of this role has grown in recent years as racists have sought to increase the longevity of their groups.

When social ties are strengthened, members who have individual identities as racist activists come to view themselves as part of a larger social movement, developing a "collective identity" of racist activism. In describing an "incubation period during which new collective identities are formed ... in submerged social networks out of view of the public eye," the sociologist Carol Mueller captures how social networks among its members support organized racism. Social ties strongly influence people to join racist movements; in addition, as members of racist groups come to know each other in social as well as activist settings, they reinforce one another's commitment to the goals of organized racism. They create the "oppositional subculture" by which organized racism is sustained over time.

Racist groups have proven remarkably successful in structuring the social lives of their adherents around movement activities. When I asked racist women how much of their socializing takes place with others in the racist movement, their estimates ranged from 50 to 100 percent, with most guessing 85 to 90 percent. As a Klanswoman told me: "Once you get into the Klan, it becomes your whole family, all your socializing, all your parties." Racist women give a variety of explanations for their predilection for spending free time among fellow racists. These include mutual protection ("a lot of people like us are afraid we will be hunted"; "we look out for one another when one is in trouble") and loyalty ("I'm totally secure in my trust in everyone in [her group]"). They also cite reinforcement of their beliefs ("I like being with people who share my beliefs"; "you do not need to defend your beliefs to anyone because they already share your views"), lack of access to other sets of friends ("when I decided I was going to be a skinhead, I lost a lot of friends, but I gained friendships I can count on"), and a perceived need for rapid and accurate sources of information ("everyone just updates on events that I should know about that are excluded from normal papers").

It is women who are responsible for making racist group life work, for creating rallies and meetings that leave people with a positive feeling. They often succeed; a skinhead remembered that her first Klan rally "was just like a big reception; it was a lot of fun." A neo-Nazi similarly recalled being surprised to find that a racist event was "kind of like a big powwow or something. There was no cross burnings or screaming."

Serving Meals

A flyer advertising a neo-Nazi event promises a day of fellowship and racist learning, along with a social time of music and meals at a local banquet hall—meals served, of course, by "the ladies." Such gendered division of labor is common among racist groups; hence, for the social hour following a strategy meeting at the Aryan Nations' racist compound in Idaho, a sixty-year-old woman played the organ and baked cookies. Although women remain in charge of providing meals for racist events in many groups, some leaders deny that such gender-specific assignments demonstrate women's marginality to racist operations. In the *Aryan Research Fellowship Newsletter*'s report on the Aryan Nations Youth Conference, a spokesman for the group claimed that women prepared meals on-site only to protect the gathered male racists, who otherwise would have had to buy meals in town (where they might fall into the hands of local police or antiracist activists).

The emphasis on survivalism and self-sufficiency in the racist movement may heighten this gendered division of labor in the future. One racist women's group sees its responsibility as "first aid, child safety, [and organizing an] emergency information guide, maternity clothes exchange, Aryan Alphabet Coloring book, Aryan Parents Newsletter, [racist] P.O.W. art collection and fund." Christian Identity women are organized as "White Nurses," preparing to heal the broken bodies of Aryan (male) combatants in the coming race war. Another group defines women's roles in the racist movement as midwifery, child care, and survival cooking. Barb, an Aryan supremacist, instructs new women recruits that "woman's big responsibility is to be ready to fight to raise children (no drop-off day camps), and be ready to offer other women a shoulder to cry on. Many young women today didn't have a parent to teach them to cook from scratch (even the generation past had that problem and turned to TV dinners); or to hand sew, and now women must learn it themselves and teach their children." The wife of a prominent Aryan supremacist was described to me by one racist skinhead woman, without intended irony, as "like Donna Reed . . . a very nice, wonderful, matronly woman." Barb is a model racist social facilitator. Her role is doggedly maternal, coaching younger skingirls in "how to make our men happy and the importance of being good parents, and make sure we're eating nutritionally, and does anyone need vitamins?" At the racist compound where she lived, this model homemaker would "have us stay and make muffins and coffee and bring them out to our men [but] she'd go through the roof if a man stepped in our flowers' cause she had these gardens all around the place."

Building Bridges

Acting as social facilitators, women are central to efforts to create links between organized racist groups and outsiders. Indeed, women's greater participation and visibility in the racist movement are probably responsible for making it more accessible to mainstream populations. Because women seem incongruous in organized racism, they lend an air of placidity to racist gatherings and seem to lessen the threat that such groups pose. Women holding babies, schooling children, or serving chicken at buffet tables can to some degree "normalize" racial politics. A journalist [Amy Benfer] recounts: "I see a Nazi sitting with a latte at an outdoor bistro table. This Nazi has no swastikas, no tattoos, no combat fatigues. Instead, she has a chic red bob, blue tinted sunglasses and a small son. If I hadn't seen her heil the Nazis at noon, I would only see a pretty mother in her early 20s enjoying the late evening sun."

Racist women acknowledge their role in this effort, noting that their involvement helps racist groups convey a sense of the ordinariness of racist activism; in the words of one woman, they "portray a positive image [of] honor and integrity." After several members of his group appeared on a TV talk show, one male racist leader commented: "The women did quite well, dressing modestly, using proper makeup and proper arguments. The men should have stayed at home."

Racist women also take more deliberate steps to gain entree into mainstream populations, seeking connections with sympathetic outsiders and attempting to recruit new members into the movement; they act as the racist equivalents of what, in her study of the African-American civil rights movement, Belinda Robnett calls "bridge leaders." A Nazi group declares its members "advocates [of] a community form of activism" and urges them to get out and meet people, so that they might show by example "the society that we would like to see." In so doing, "we will do much to break the image that the Zionist controlled news media portrays about white nationalists." Among the varieties of community involvement suggested are "running for public office, engaging in business, and generally acting as responsible citizens, all while being openly known as National Socialists."

Promoting Other Causes

Many neo-Nazi and Klan groups practice some form of community "outreach." One woman described the work of women in her group on behalf of animal protection, which they support as an affirmation of "mother nature" against the masculine "cowardly excuse for power called 'sport killing,' . . . the need in their pitiful lives to establish a sense of dominance." Some go further, claiming environmentalism and animal rights as issues for white racist activists since "it is not necessary to carry on a race if there is not a world to live in." Such efforts, along with programs in self-education, first aid, and survival cooking, are described by a member as "projects that bring respect in the community so they'll listen."

Racist women understand that groups of women who seem innocuous can attract people into racist politics. They are fully aware that most people enter the racist movement through personal contacts with existing members, and they work to create the opportunities that make such recruitment possible. Bible study groups bring ordinary women into contact with hard-core racists. Animal rights turn into Aryan rights. One recruit told of attending a women's meeting billed as a Christian apocalyptic "preparation for end times"; she thought that "it would be boring—but it turned out to be excellent and exciting, with all the women who participated (and most did) taking part and exchanging ideas, really great." Although she expressed disappointment that "many things listed were not covered in depth due to time running down," the list of topics shows a strategic mixture of fundamentalist Christianity, self-sufficiency, and racism, with lessons on women in Scriptures, home birthing, healing with herbs, and home schooling tucked between workshops on "how to use the system" and revelations about domestic spy satellites and secret inoculations with microscopic "transformers" meant to "track our people." Perhaps the greatest threat posed by modern organized racism is seen not in the highly visible parades of middle-aged Klan members, who are inevitably far outnumbered by anti-Klan demonstrators, but in the mundane advertisements for toddler car seats and Aryan cookbooks that appear in white-power newsletters and on Aryan electronic bulletin boards.

10

Women are Gaining Leadership Roles in White Nationalist Organizations

Lisa Turner with Russ Nieli

At the time if this interview, Lisa Turner was the Woman's Information Coordinator for the World Church of the Creator. Her interviewer, Russ Nieli, is a lecturer at Princeton University. He and Professor Swain are opposed to White Supremacy.

Lisa Turner believes the white race is nature's finest creation. As Women's Information Coordinator for the Church of the Creator, an anti-Christian white supremacy group, Turner uses the Internet to recruit like-minded individuals to pro-white activism. In the Church, men and women have distinct roles. Turner sees her mission as the protection of the white race.

INTERVIEWER: You are the Women's Information Coordinator for the World Church of the Creator, an organization that espouses an atheistic and white supremacist religious philosophy known as Creativity. Could you explain what the Creativity religion is and how you first became interested in it?

TURNER: Well, basically Creativity states that the white race is nature's finest creation, that through looking at the lessons of history, through commonsense, and through our own powers of observation, we can see that the white race has accomplished the most, has invented the most, has been indeed the most productive and creative race on the face of the earth. The members of the World Church of the Creator are called Creators, because we believe that we have indeed brought forth the highest and finest creations.

My involvement with the World Church of the Creator came about through a contact with [white supremacist leader] Rev. Matt Hale over the Internet. Prior to that time, I had not been a formal member of any prowhite organization, and when I came into contact with him, he introduced me to the racial religion of Creativity. The Creativity religion seemed to express more clearly than anything else I had ever encountered before exactly what I felt the white race should be following and should be adhering to—which is getting away from the Jewish pollution of our race through the Biblical fantasies of Christianity, which we believe have led our race to destruction. The central tenets of Creativity really appealed to me. I had never been very interested in being part of what they call the Christian Identity movement, so I started reading the primary books of Creativity, such as *Nature's Eternal Religion*, which is one of the main books that was written by our founder, Ben Klassen, and I was very impressed by what he had to say. I therefore joined the church formally in March of 1998. Besides Klassen's work, I was extremely impressed by Rev. Hale in terms of his leadership ability. I felt he was a very charismatic, magnetic person who really had the capacity to lead our people to victory and make a real impact in today's prowhite scene. . . .

Working for the Church

INTERVIEWER: What are your responsibilities as Women's Information Coordinator for the World Church of the Creator? What sort of things do you do on behalf of your church?

TURNER: One of my primary activities is to make use of the Internet whenever I can as a way of networking among like-minded individuals to recruit women to the church. I also have a monthly newsletter called *The Women's Frontier*, which is a very powerful medium to get the word out. We have around 700 to 800 subscribers now to the newsletter. The other most powerful device that I have is the Women's Frontier website, which was established, I guess, around a couple of months after I joined the church. I started one of the most advanced women's websites on the entire Internet, and I make heavy use of it as a recruiting device. So those are the two primary ways that I recruit and put the message out of Creativity.

Women must be included as partners—not as equals in the sense that we are the same as men, but partners in this struggle. . . .

The Role of Women

INTERVIEWER: You are something of an anomaly among members of groups that espouse white supremacy insofar as you are a woman. Most other white supremacy organizations seem to attract mainly males and hold traditionalist views regarding the subordinate role of women. Could you explain your views regarding the role of women both in society at large and in the white supremacy movement? Does the World Church of the Creator affirm a male leadership principle or is it acceptable for women to assume leadership positions in the group?

TURNER: Well, first of all, I should explain that we view men and women as being different. We believe that nature's laws should be adhered to in that men have their own special role to play, and so do women. We believe that women's most important role is as wives and mothers to white children. We certainly, though, encourage women to take on leadership roles. Obviously, I am in a leadership position within the church. We encourage women to be all that they can be and do all that they can do, and we do not seek to limit women. However, this is not a feminist stance. We still recognize that women are going to look at things differently than men do and take a different approach. Women tend to be more nurturing. We tend to be more diplomatic in some cases, and we celebrate the difference between men and women.

[W]e have women from all walks of life who join the church. But I would say that they are still predominantly in the eighteen- to twenty-five-year-old age group.

But, we do encourage women to assume leadership roles in the church. Women within the church can become reverends, just as the men can, if they take the ministerial exam. Women can lead their own church meetings and head up Women's Frontier chapters. So we don't seek to segregate women from men in the church, and we give a woman who has leadership qualities every bit as much respect as we would a man who shows such qualities. This is different, I suppose, from some of the other prowhite organizations. We believe those other organizations are reactionary in their views in attempting to hold women back and to restrict their roles. We don't think that's going to bring victory to our cause. It's really counterproductive for white women to stand on the sidelines and not fight side by side with their male comrades, and we feel very strongly that if other groups and organizations are going to continue to take that tack, that they will never see the kind of victory that they want. It's like trying to run a race with one leg. You can't do it. Women must be included as partners—not as equals in the sense that we are the same as men, but partners in this struggle—and more and more people in our cause are beginning to understand that and recognize that. I receive probably hundreds of e-mails, mainly from men, who say that they are thrilled to see that women are finally having a voice, that they are coming forward. I would say that 80 percent of subscribers on my mailing list are men.

So we have had overwhelming support from men, and we are very proud of the accomplishments that we've made.

Demographics

INTERVIEWER: Is it conceivable that a woman would ever become head of the World Church of the Creator?

TURNER: The head position, the pontifex maximus, in the World Church of the Creator is reserved to a man but only for one reason, and that is that we view the top role of leadership as being analogous to the head of the family, which we do see as the male's role. So we see the pontifex as being like the head of our church family, and we do restrict that to a male. However, the next position in line to pontifex, which is hasta primus, and is analogous to a vice president, is open to a woman.

INTERVIEWER: What sort of women join the World Church of the Creator? What demographic groups do you recruit from and what reasons do women have for joining your organization?

TURNER: Well, we have women from all walks of life who join the church. But I would say that they are still predominantly in the eighteen- to twenty-five-year-old age group. We would like to broaden our horizons, but there are women from all ages who join the church, and I don't want to perpetuate a stereotype and say that it's just young women or women from a certain economic background who join, because that's not true. I myself have a college degree, a B.A., and we have many college-educated women coming into the church. We are trying to do a lot more college outreach on the campuses, so we do hope to expand the demographics in that way. But I'm not going to say that it's any one particular age group or economic background that joins. I receive mail from all kinds of wome—young women, middle-aged women, working class women, women who have professional degrees—so it's really all over the map.

College Outreach

INTERVIEWER: How successful have you been with the college outreach?

TURNER: Well, we feel that we have been moderately successful. We distribute a great deal of literature on the campuses. I have heard from a girl who is a student at Cornell, I have heard from other students from other Ivy League campuses. One of the problems in that arena, of course, is that there is still a sense of stigma and persecution. Some women are a little bit afraid about coming out and being openly prowhite, so it may be a little difficult for us right now to completely gauge just how many supporters we have on the campuses. We feel that there is a great deal of support; it's just a question of convincing them that what they have to do is stand up for our race and not be intimidated by campus administrators. This is something that we are going to do a lot more targeting of in the next year. . . .

[M]y mission in life . . . is to bring more racial awareness to white women because I believe that white women have been used as pawns by the Jewish power structure in this country.

On a Mission

INTERVIEWER: That ends our formal questions. Is there anything else that you would like to tell us that you haven't already talked about, or something that you said but would like to expand upon or reinforce?

TURNER: Yes, I would like to explain again that the most important mission or goal that I have is the recruitment of women, and that is where I spend most of my time, and most of my energies. My overall goal, my mission in life, is to bring more racial awareness to white women because I believe that white women have been used as pawns by the Jewish power structure in this country. They have been co-opted into believing that they somehow have something in common with quote "the minorities." I wrote an essay that was probably considered the most popular piece that I have written—it was reprinted in *Spearhead* magazine for the British Nationalist Party—which was called "The Co-optation of White Women." I made clear in that essay how women have been brainwashed and propagandized into being foot soldiers in the war against the white male. I wrote the essay because I got sick and tired every time I picked up a newspaper and women would be included in this laundry list of individuals . . . illegal aliens, racial minorities, dysfunctional people, blah-blah, and women—as if women were part of this army of nonwhites and dysfunctionals against the white male. I wanted to make clear that women are part of that. We white women are sick and tired of being included with quote "the minorities." We're not a minority. We're here to fight beside our white male comrades with pride and dignity, and I'm very, very proud of a lot of the breakthroughs that the Women's Frontier has made. It is one of the few women's organizations in the entire prowhite movement. You may have heard of Women for Aryan Unity in Canada, but we're still part of only a handful of women's organizations. I hope to see the prowhite movement grow and expand, and we will continue to spearhead this growth. I'm very excited to be a part of what I consider history in the making, and I want women to finally recognize just how they have been used. More and more white women are waking up and understanding that they have been used by the Jew power structure, and to bring about this continued awareness is my primary goal and mission within the church.

11

Behind an Innocent Facade White Supremacist Singers Spread Hate

Earl Ofari Hutchinson

Journalist and author Earl Ofari Hutchinson writes on the African American experience. His nine books include The Assassination of the Black Male Image *and* Black Fatherhood: The Guide to Male Parenting.

Fourteen-year-old twins Lamb and Lynx Gaede, who form the duo Prussian Blue, are the new face of white supremacist music. They mix teen chatter and patriotism with a rock beat, along with pleas for white pride. In addition to being popular with white supremacists, their musical mix and innocent persona allows the sisters to spread a message of hate beyond its usual audience. Lamb and Lynx's music raises concern among antiracism groups, who worry that their cute appearance will serve to hide the coded racism they seek to spread.

Last October, ABC News profiled 14-year-old twin sisters Lamb and Lynx Gaede and their white supremacist band Prussian Blue. It branded them the new musical spokes-kids for white supremacy—which ignited rage and disgust in their hometown of Bakersfield, California.

The sisters' mother said she wanted a whiter place to live, and moved to Kalispell, Montana. That didn't quiet the furor. A group of enraged townspeople are now circulating flyers headed, "No Hate Here" and demanding that the family pack up and leave.

Earl Ofari Hutchinson, "Music to Hate By," *New American Media*, September 20, 2006. news.newamericanmedia.org. Reproduced by permission.

That may or may not be a good thing. After all, as odious as their hate message is, the twins and their mom have the right to say and sing what they want. But even if they were given the swift boot from town, their music and the influence they may have over some impressionable and naïve white 13- to 19-year-old teens (their target audience) can't easily be booted away.

Prussian Blue pumps their music through the 24-hour Internet Radio White and other websites. The sites feature more than 5,000 youth-oriented white supremacist songs on their playlists. They market their songs through record labels and websites.

The twins cleverly mix personal, introspective, giggly teen chatter in their lyrics, along with patriotic appeals to fight for freedom, to a stomp-down toe-tapping rock beat. That appeals to the musical tastes of many youth. The songs can easily be slipped into an MP3 player and listened to away from the prying ears of adults.

The twins' lyrical deception is crucial in order to sell their race-baiting ideology to teens. . . . They use racial and gender-inferred double speak, code words and code concepts.

In "I Will Bleed For You," for example, they make a plea for pride and dignity: "Have you no pride in your heritage, and no pride in your name. I'm glad that I'm not like you. I know my children are proud of me. Mine will always stay free."

Appealing to Young, White Girls

White supremacist groups quickly spotted a good thing in Prussian Blue. A critic on the National Vanguard website gushed over the release of the group's second album, "The Stranger." He hailed it as the first white nationalist album that appeals to young (white) girls. The potential tap of the main-stream alternative rock market potentially could translate into millions of listeners and thousands of sales.

The twins' lyrical deception is crucial in order to sell their race-baiting ideology to teens. Much of the public frowns on the crude racism and anti-Semitism of the old Klan. Racial and gender slurs and assaults against minorities, women, gays and feminists are considered publicly impolite. And white supremacist groups have adjusted to the times. They borrow the technique politicians perfected during the past quarter century to win white votes. They use racial and gender-inferred double speak, code words and code concepts.

In the 1960's, it was law and order, crime in the streets, rampant permissiveness, and out-of-touch federal bureaucrats. In the 1970s it was high taxes, crime and OPEC. In the 1980s and 1990s it was heavy-handed government, welfare cheats, drug dealers and gang bangers.

The federal government is an omnipresent force for Americans. White supremacist groups have transformed the government into an evil instrument that wrings hard earned tax dollars from the shrinking incomes of the white middle-class. The money, they rail, goes to subsidize welfare scamming women, crime prone-blacks and Latinos and assorted social and gender deviants. Many white males are gripped by the ultra-paranoid delusion that the government conspires with minorities, women and the poor to marginalize them.

Oklahoma City bomber Timothy McVeigh punched all the code buttons in angry letters in 1992. He railed against crime, high taxes, corrupt politicians, government mismanagement and the "eroding American Dream." McVeigh made only a passing comment on race and nothing on gender. It wasn't necessary.

The new breed white supremacist groups are also helped by the storehouse of dodge tactics many Americans employ to mask racism. They accuse blacks of always "making an issue out of race." They avoid having any physical or personal contact with blacks. They get angry or defensive when racial issues are raised. They resist programs for ostensibly non-racial reasons that they perceive directly or indirectly benefit minorities.

Soft-Sell Hate

The immigration reform battle has created a fertile new field for white supremacy groups to slip in their race- coded bigotry, and corral new recruits. They play on the anxiety and fears of many American over illegal immigration, and cloak their message of white purity in a call to defend the borders and halt an alleged alien invasion. The Southern Poverty Law Center which tracks 700 hate groups, in its latest *Intelligence Report* notes a jump in the number of threats and outright physical attacks on Hispanics. The Klan, Neo-Nazis and racist skinheads have also staged anti-immigration rallies and marches. The twins appeared at one of those rallies and sported "Stop Immigration" t-shirts.

Prussian Blue's disarming lyrics and soft-sale marketing has touched off warning bells among the Anti-Defamation League and other groups that monitor hate groups. They warn school officials to be on the alert for sneaky efforts by the hate groups to recruit youth through catchy rock songs. The popularity and deadly innocence of two 14-year-old singers give the warning even more urgency.

12

Christian Identity's Bizarre Beliefs Lead to Extreme Violence

Anti-Defamation League

The Anti-Defamation League of the B'nai Brith is an organization dedicated to combating anti-semitism, racism, and other forms of discrimination and hate.

Christian Identity is an obscure but virulent belief system whose origins date back to nineteenth-century England. Its basic tenet is that white Europeans are the descendants of the lost tribes of Israel, and thus represent God's true chosen people. People of other races are a lesser type of human being, according to Christian Identity. The belief system was not originally anti-Semitic, but in the 1930s became so when its leaders concocted a story that the Jews were descended from the snake in the biblical Garden of Eden story. Christian Identity attracts extreme white supremacists, many of whom have committed violent crime. Since the 1980s, believers have been implicated in a series of domestic terrorism incidents.

One of the most remarkable developments in the extreme right in the United States in the past few decades has been the rise of an obscure religious ideology known as Christian Identity. Penetrating existing racist and anti-Semitic groups and movements, it has inflamed their bigotry with religious fervor and also sparked the creation of many new

Anti-Defamation League, "Christian Identity," *Extremism in America*, 2005. www.adl .org.

groups. Adherents have committed hate crimes, bombings and other acts of terrorism. Identity's current influence ranges from Ku Klux Klan and neo-Nazi groups to the anti-government militia and sovereign citizen movements—yet most Americans are unaware that it even exists.

The "Lost Tribes" Found

Christian Identity's origins can be traced back to the nineteenth century in Great Britain, where a small circle of religious thinkers advanced the idea, known as British-Israelism or Anglo-Israelism, that modern Europeans were biologically descended from the ancient Israelites of the Old Testament—specifically, from the "Lost Tribes" scattered by invasions of Hittites, Assyrians and Babylonians. The Lost Tribes had purportedly made their way to Europe, and from them descended the modern European nationalities.

These peculiar views—arrived at through creative interpretation of scripture, language, and history never became widely popular. According to Michael Barkun, the leading historian of Christian Identity, the British-Israel movement in Great Britain peaked in the 1920s with approximately five thousand adherents. Although eccentric, British-Israelites seem to have had no ambitious political agenda or animus, and were probably no more racist or anti-Semitic than the mainstream of Western culture at that time.

Once on American shores, British-Israelism began to evolve. Originally, believers viewed contemporary Jews as descendants of those ancient Israelites who had never been "lost." They might be seen critically but, given their significant role in the British-Israel genealogical scheme, not usually with animosity. By the 1930s, however, in the U.S., a strain of anti-Semitism started to permeate the movement (though some maintained traditional beliefs—and a small number of traditionalists still exist in the U.S.).

Taking hold in this country at a time when anti-Semitism was as well, British Israelism increasingly advanced the idea—common in anti-Semitic circles in the early twentieth century—that most Jews were not really descendants of ancient Israelites, but were instead descended from an Asiatic people known as the Khazars, who settled near the Black Sea during the Middle Ages. European (Ashkenazic) Jews were thus "false" Israelites who further obscured the fact that it was really white Europeans who were the "true" Israelites. . . .

An Ugly Turn

The anti-Semitic strain of British-Israelism was particularly strong on the West Coast of Canada and the United States. The key figure in the transformation of British-Israelism into what was increasingly called "Christian Identity" was Wesley Swift (1913–1970), a former Methodist minister from Southern California. In the 1940s, Swift started his own church, later known as the Church of Jesus Christ Christian. He was active in extreme right-wing groups, including the Ku Klux Klan, and developed a close friendship with the nation's most prominent postwar anti-Semite, Gerald L. K. Smith. Because of the activities of Swift and associates such as Bertrand Comparet and San Jacinto Capt, Christian Identity increasingly became linked with extreme right-wing ideologies. . . .

The core of the system, as with British-Israelism, was that white Europeans were descended from the Israelite people of the Bible: this was their true "identity." Volumes of identity writing is devoted to revealing this hidden history. As anti-Semitism came to be folded into these accounts, the result was a fanciful but ostensibly Biblical rationale for hatred of Jews.

The most extreme expression of identity anti-Semitism is the so-called "two-seed" (or "seedliner") theory, developed by Swift, his associates and his disciples in the 1960s. According to the two-seed theory, the seduction of Eve by the Serpent in Eden was sexual, Cain was the product of their liaison and

Cain, in turn, was the father of the Jewish people; all Jews, therefore, are children of the devil, literally demonic. The other seedline in the two-seed scheme traces from Adam and Eve's other son, Abel, through the lost tribes to today's white European-derived believers. . . .

Another significant aspect of Christian Identity theology is its millennialism—the belief that the world is in its final days. Millennialism is widespread among Protestants around the world, but Identity diverges sharply from traditional forms of Protestantism. Like many evangelicals, Christian Identity adherents believe that Jesus Christ will return to the Earth following a period of "tribulation." However, Identity adherents reject the popular evangelical contention that devoted followers of Jesus will be "saved" or "raptured" before the Tribulation begins (a concept known as premillennialism). Identity is postmillennial: it holds that Jesus will not return until after the Tribulation. Many believe they are in or are about to enter into the time of Tribulation, a great battle between good and evil in which they will take part. While some Protestants are also postmillennial, Identity Christians view the apocalypse as a racial battle, which helps to create a hothouse atmosphere wherever Identity thrives.

Christian Identity's racist and apocalyptic qualities helped lead to several well-known incidents of domestic terrorism during the past quarter century.

Because they believe in the imminent collapse of worldly institutions, Identity adherents tend to devalue and distrust secular institutions in ways that make extreme anti-government ideologies (such as those of militia groups or sovereign citizens) appealing. They hold themselves to "God's laws," not "man's laws," and many do not feel bound to a government that they consider run by Jews, the New World Order or some other sinister entity. This anti-secularism has led to reclusiveness among Identity Christians, with some living by themselves or with like-minded people in isolated locations (such as the "Elohim City" compound in eastern Oklahoma). . . .

A Movement Develops

Christian Identity penetrated most of the major extreme-right movements. Thanks to Aryan Nations, some neo-Nazis became believers. Klan leaders such as Thomas Robb and Louis Beam adopted the faith, as did some racist skinheads, such as the Hammerskins. Christian Identity also found a welcome home in extreme anti-government activism, notably the tax protest movement, the sovereign citizen movement (descended from Gale's Posse Comitatus) and the militia movement. The resurgence of right-wing extremism in the 1990s following the Ruby Ridge and Waco standoffs further spread Identity beliefs.

The influence of Identity often extends beyond Identity circles. The Militia of Montana, which helped create the militia movement, is headed by Identity adherents, though they do not promote the theology. Similarly, one of the most popular anti-government magazines, *Media Bypass*, was recently purchased by the Identity journalists Chris Temple and Paul Hall, Jr., who have so far only rarely injected Identity messages into the magazine's anti-government, conspiratorial contents.

At the start of the 21st century, Christian Identity is strongest in the Pacific Northwest and the Midwest, but Christian Identity groups or churches can be found in virtually every region of the United States (outside the United States, it is much weaker, but there are Identity groups in Canada, Ireland, Great Britain, Australia and South Africa). Yet while spread far it is also spread thin. Estimates of the total number of believers in North America vary from a low of 25,000 to a high of 50,000; the true number is probably closer to the low end of the scale. Given this relatively small following, its extensive penetration of the far right is all the more remarkable. . . .

Violence and Hate

Christian Identity's racist and apocalyptic qualities helped lead to several well-known incidents of domestic terrorism during the past quarter century. In North Dakota in 1983, Gordon Kahl demonstrated how radical Identity adherents could be when he killed two U.S. Marshals who had come to arrest him for a parole violation (a mourner at one funeral was Assistant Attorney General Rudolph W. Giuliani, later to become all too familiar with such funerals). A four-month manhunt ended in another shootout in Arkansas, where Kahl killed a local sheriff before he himself was killed.

That same year, the white supremacist terrorist group known as The Order began its series of armed robberies (to which it would add additional crimes ranging from counterfeiting to assassination). Several members of the gang were Christian Identity, including David Tate, who in 1985 killed a Missouri State Highway Patrol officer attempting to reach an Identity survivalist compound called the Covenant, the Sword, and the Arm of the Lord (CSA). An ensuing standoff resulted in the demise of the CSA and the arrest of its leadership. During the 1980s, several Identity groups attempted to follow in the footsteps of The Order, including The Order II and the Arizona Patriots, who committed bombings and an attempted armored car robbery, respectively.

Crime Continues

In the 1990s, Identity criminal activity continued apace, including efforts by an Oklahoma Identity minister, Willie Ray Lampley, to commit a series of bombings in the summer of 1995 in the wake of the Oklahoma City bombing by Timothy McVeigh. The following year, the Montana Freemen, whose leaders were Identity, made headlines for their "paper terrorism" tactics and their 81-day standoff with the federal government. In 1998, Eric Rudolph, who had been associated with Identity ministers such as Nord Davis and Dan Gayman, became a fugitive after allegedly bombing gay bars, the Atlanta Summer Olympics, and an abortion clinic. The following year, Buford Furrow, a former Aryan Nations security guard, went on a shooting spree at a Jewish Community Center in Los Angeles, wounding four children and an adult, and later killing a Filipino-American postal worker.

Perhaps the most chilling manifestation of Identity terrorism can be found in the concept of the Phineas Priesthood, set forth by Richard Kelly Hoskins in his 1990 book *Vigilantes of Christendom*. The Priesthood is based on the concept of the obscure Biblical character Phinehas, an Israelite who used a spear to slay a "race-mixing" fellow Israelite and the Midianite woman with whom he had sex. Hoskins conjured up the idea of an elite class of "Phineas Priests," self-anointed warriors who would use extreme measures to attack race-mixers, gays, or abortionists, among other targets. Over the years, some have committed crimes using the Phineas Priest label, including a group of about eight who committed bombings and bank robberies in the Spokane, Washington, area in 1996 (four of whom were caught and sentenced to lengthy prison terms). In 2002, two Aryan Nations splinter groups openly adopted Phineas Priest names or symbols.

13

White Racialists Should Lead Honorable White Lives

Robert S. Griffin

Robert S. Griffin is Professor of Education at the University of Vermont. He is a racially conscious author whose works include the book The Fame of a Dead Man's Deeds: An Up-Close Portrait of White Nationalist William Pierce.

White racialists are rightfully concerned with the state of society and the nation as a whole; however, if they allow these concerns to take up too much of their attention, they risk neglecting the "small picture," that is, living honorable white lives. An honorable white lifestyle has certain characteristics. To be true to themselves—and have happier and more fulfilling lives—white racialists should try to live by these standards.

The living white perspective, or construct, shines a light on the nature and quality of the lives of individual white people—this one, that one, and that one over there, and you and me. How are we doing? Day to day, month to month, year to year, are we doing what is natural and right for us? Are we living with integrity, in alignment with our deepest insights and highest values? Are we living proudly and openly and courageously? Are we getting important things done? Are we healthy and happy? Are we loved and supported? Are we living honorable white lives?

Robert S. Griffin, "Living White: A Personal Challenge and Responsibility," *The Occidental Quarterly*, vol. 2, no. 4, Winter 2002. Reproduced by permission. http://theoccidentalquarterly.com.

The "Small Picture" Needs More Attention

This concern for the circumstance of individual white men and women and boys and girls reflects a "small picture" in contrast to a "big picture" frame of reference, the latter being more abstract, theoretical, and impersonal. By big picture I mean analyses of what is happening in society overall, what is going on politically, what ideas and ways ought to prevail in the culture, that sort of thing. In this white racial area, a big picture orientation might result in a consideration of what is happening with immigration in America, or interracial crime, or white nationalist political strategies. At least potentially, small picture and big picture orientations are complementary, each informing and completing the other. The ideal, it seems to me, is a white racialist worldview that harmoniously integrates "all-of-it"—matters of history, philosophy, analyses of the cultural and social context, visions of the future of the race, and so on—with "one-of-it," which concerns the fates of particular, mortal white men, women, and children.

I see an imbalance at the moment, however: namely, too much focus on the big picture at the expense of the small picture. That is to say, I think we are better at talking about how it all works than how our individual lives work. My worry is that without greater attention to what I am calling living white—specific and realistic personal goals and down-to-earth, practical strategies and actions for achieving those goals—too many racially conscious white people will end up talkers rather than doers, and feel okay about that. Too many will become reviewers, commentators, spectators in life, rather than participants. Too many will come to assume that circumstances in the world and in their own lives are bigger than they can do anything about, and as a consequence they will live lives characterized more by coping and hiding out than by honest self-expression. Too many will live with a significant discrepancy between what they know and value and the way they conduct their lives, and this will gnaw at them and, over time, take its personal toll on them. Too many will have lives that are more frustrating than gratifying—"knowing the score" and "talking a good game" are poor substitutes for living with dignity.

Living White

Thus I think it advisable to give greater attention to the manner in which actual white people conduct their lives. My assumption is that there are ways of living that grow out of white people's basic nature and cultural heritage. If that is so, if there is an approach to life that is natural to us, consistent with who we are, what is it? What does it mean to live white? What does it mean for whites collectively, and—the concern here—what does it mean for an individual? How does an individual answer that question for himself, or herself? And after answering it—or anyway, resolving it—the question becomes, is she or he actually managing live that way? Is he or she getting it done? Getting it done involves figuring this out, concretely, and then implementing it successfully. It involves getting from hopes to reality. Goal achievement capability is crucially important: Living an honorable white life takes more than insight and good intentions; it takes efficacy, the ability to make things happen in one's own life. It takes "how-to" capability. Another way to put it: The white racialist movement needs a technology of personal change to complement its ideological positions and social and cultural analyses and programs.

White persons are born with a particular genetic makeup. They grow up and live as adults, amid particular influences, prominent among them their racial and cultural heritage, their parents and other relatives, friends, and acquaintances, their church, neighborhood, and school, the contemporary social and cultural circumstance, and the mass media. They find mates and some work to do and a place to live. They create a family and rear children. They take part in leisure activities.

They engage the larger world—organizations, politics, the public discourse. They experience success and failure, love and satisfaction, pain and regret. They get sick and get well and then get sick and die, leaving whatever mark on posterity they do. The idea of living white says to each of us: This is the playing field of your life. Work within this context and fashion an honorable life as a white man or woman.

I believe that happiness results from doing what you ought to do, and white people ought to live true to their heritage.

Characteristics of an Honorable White Lifestyle

There isn't just one way to be an honorable white person, but I propose honorable white lives have some common characteristics:

1. There is a strong sense of *racial identity and pride.*

2. There is a strong sense of *racial commitment,* a dedication to live in accordance with the highest ideals or standards of the white race.

3. There is a sense of *racial responsibility* to one's racial brethren.

4. There is *racial integrity.* There is a tight fit between the individual's highest racial convictions and actions. A tight fit, not a perfect fit; life isn't perfect, but there is a good correspondence between one's racial beliefs and one's deeds.

5. There is *courage and toughness.* These days, the world is very unfriendly to people with a strong white racial consciousness, to the point that it would do them in if it could. Living white requires fortitude, and it requires hardness and resilience. Living white means being fierce when it's called for and knowing how to fight and being willing to do it.

6. There is *physical and mental health*. You can't get it done if you are dragging physically—tired, washed out, overweight, half sick, and addicted to one thing or another, as so many people are, even those who are considered to be in good health. And you can't get it done if inner demons call the shots and lead you off into the marshes.

7. There is a *positive mental attitude*. Unfortunately, the most highly developed capability among many white racialists is identifying how somebody else (and often that somebody else is another white racialist) is wrong or messed up, and being pessimistic and cynical—a sure ticket to personal stagnation and inner upheaval.

8. There is *efficacy* (how-to capability). You can't live with integrity and responsibility if you are unable to get good things done. Significant accomplishment is necessary to living white. Significant accomplishment doesn't have to mean altering American foreign policy in the Middle East. It can mean getting good results with your children. It can mean finding work that allows you to express your values and live more honestly. It can mean creating a living space that reflects who you truly are. Efficacy comes down to the ability to set tangible, imaginable, realizable objectives and take effective action to achieve those goals. Some people seem to know everything about everything, but when they try to do something they come up short. Others seem to spend all their time weighing options and making plans that they will implement when the time is right, but the time is never right.

9. And a last characteristic common to those living an honorable white life: *personal happiness*. By personal happiness I mean a basic sense of satisfaction, gratification. It is the experience of "Yes, life is good." Indeed, there are pain and loss and downtimes, as there are in

every life, but pervading it all is the conclusion, "I'm living the life I should live." Amid the struggles and setbacks, and outweighing them by far, is victory and self-respect and peace of mind. I believe that happiness results from doing what you ought to do, and white people ought to live true to their heritage. If you don't, if you live with major incongruities between how you conduct your life and who you are at the core of your being, you may have cars and houses and worldly acclaim and people who admire and love you, but still, deep down, you won't experience real happiness.

Talking with Others about Living White

Below, I'll describe five outcomes that have resulted for me from looking at things through the lens of living white. I hope this list encourages readers to identify concerns and projects related to their own interests and circumstances.

First, I have been prompted to talk to other people about what it means to live white. Here's one example from a recent e-mail exchange: "My thoughts on the 'white way of life,'" my correspondent offered, "are that there's a quietness, an industriousness and a graciousness about it. Whites tend to their gardens, work in their fields, chop wood, walk their dogs, smoke their pipes, write their letters and read their books. They make things with their hands. They speak softly. I see this in rural, suburban, and urban settings. This may come as a surprise to you, but one good example of this is Garrison Keillor's radio program on NPR. Keillor features white folk music and wistful tales of this character and that: the parson and his failed romance, the football star who became principal, the spinster librarian and her delicious apple pies. Keillor doesn't glorify high-flying capitalists and violent rap stars but rather celebrates modesty, frugality, peacefulness, and respect for natural forces. Keillor captures the white spirit well: sturdy values, gentle humor, matter-of-factness, church socials, calm perseverance, enjoyment of the simple things really, the joys and sweet sorrows of life on earth, in a community of white racial kin." And then in reply to my response to what he said: "When I referred to 'high-flying capitalist.' I was thinking of a race-traitor type, snorting cocaine in his high-priced Manhattan apartment, with no morals and no loyalty to racial kin, who is bent on enriching himself whatever the cost to anyone or anything else. And I absolutely agree with you that adventurism, artistic intensity, and entrepreneurship are part of what it means to be white. I was just expressing my new-found skepticism of the materialistic individualism promoted by globalist conservatives and libertarians—a crew I once found myself attracted to."

Second, I am finishing up a book made up of the personal accounts of fifteen racially conscious white people, *One Sheaf, One Vine: Fifteen White Americans Talk About Race*. The title comes from a Rudyard Kipling poem, *The Stranger*:

Let the corn be all one sheaf—

and the grapes be all one vine,

Ere our children's teeth are set on
edge

By bitter bread and wine.

Community Building

Third, I've thought about the possibilities of a Living White website devoted to practical, how-to-do-it matters, with postings, articles, and links. "I don't like what is happening to my neighborhood and have heard about inexpensive land in Kentucky and building 'backwoods' homes. Where can I learn more about that?" "How do I make my work more reflective of what I believe?" "How can I pass on their heritage to my children?" "How can I get tougher?" (I am reminded of a comment by a white racialist: "If you are going to be one of us, you have to be willing to fight up close.") "Is there anything I can do about my children's education besides home-schooling? Is a Waldorf school a good possibility?" "How do I get politically involved?"

The living white idea says we need to turn away from the big issues facing the race long enough to ask ... "In the way I am conducting my life, what do I exemplify racially, what do I further racially?"

Fourth, many racially conscious whites feel isolated and unsupported. Another e-mail acquaintance put it this way: "How can I make some local connections? I feel a need to communicate and collaborate with like-minded folk. I want to be around a healthy Euro way of life that is continuing and growing, where kids are embracing their heritage and its lore and its music." In response to this and similar statements, I have thought about the possibility of what I am calling at this point White Honor Clubs. The idea would be to have local clubs whose purpose is to support members in their efforts to live honorable white lives. It could be a place for social exchange and networking, and for idea sharing and advice giving and mutual support. It could be a place to discuss how to find a good place to live or work that is consistent with your racial ideals, or how to raise and educate children, or how to stand up to the pressure to conform to ideas and ways that are contrary to your racial beliefs. It could be a place to get more informed—books to read, web sites to visit, people to contact, etc.—and stronger personally. It could be a place to identify constructive things to do. It could be a place to identify and undertake collaborative projects, say, in response to some local issue. All to say that a White Honor Club would be about the well-being of the people in the room.

Improving Ourselves

Fifth, over the last five years, and increasingly the past year or so, I have personally tried to move in the directions that I

101

outlined in the last section—toward greater racial identity and integrity, toward courage and health and a more positive mental attitude. I am living a truer life now than before, and, indeed, I'm happier now than I was.

The living white idea says that if we want to improve the world we need to improve ourselves. It says that we need to go beyond knowing the way and pointing the way to *being* the way. It is not enough for us to understand what is going on in the world and to advocate the right things. The measure of us as individual human beings is the extent to which we engage in a quest to live consistently with what is deepest within us and are least reasonably successful at it. The living white idea says we need to turn away from the big issues facing the race long enough to ask, "What am I doing with my time on this earth? In the way I am conducting my life, what do I exemplify racially, what do I further racially? What are some tangible things I can do to live a more honorable white life?" The living white idea says that whatever answer we come to in response to the last of these questions, the one about what I can do, we need to get about doing those things—and not tomorrow, *today.*

Organizations to Contact

The editors have compiled the following list of organizations concerned with the issues debated in this book. The descriptions are derived from materials provided by the organizations. All have publications or information available for interested readers. The list was compiled on the date of publication of the present volume; the information provided here may change. Be aware that many organizations take several weeks or longer to respond to inquiries, so allow as much time as possible.

American Civil Liberties Union (ACLU)
125 Broad St., 18th Fl., New York, NY   10004-2400
(800) 775-ACLU (2258)
Web site: www.aclu.org

The American Civil Liberties Union (ACLU) is a national organization that works to defend Americans' civil rights as guaranteed by the U.S. Constitution. This has, at times, placed it on either side of the white supremacy issue, as it has advocated for the rights of minorities as well as defended the rights of white supremacists to freedom of speech and assembly. The ACLU publishes and distributes policy statements, pamphlets, and the semiannual newsletter *Civil Liberties Alert*.

Amnesty International (AI)
5 Penn Plaza, 14th Fl., New York, NY   10001
(212) 807-8400 • fax: (212) 463-9193
e-mail: admin-us@aiusa.org
Web site: www.amnesty.org

Founded in 1961, Amnesty International (AI) is a grassroots activist organization that aims to free all nonviolent people who have been imprisoned because of their beliefs, ethnic origin, sex, color, or language. The *Amnesty International Report* is published annually, and other reports are available online and by mail.

Anti-Defamation League (ADL)

823 United Nations Plaza, New York, NY   10017
(212) 490-2525
Web site: www.adl.org

The Anti-Defamation League (ADL) works to stop the defamation of Jews and to ensure fair treatment for all U.S. citizens. It publishes the periodic *ADL Law Report* and *Law Enforcement Bulletin* as well as other reports. It has an active project to train police organizations to recognize hate crimes, and promotes the passing of anti-hate crime legislation.

Center for the Study of Popular Culture (CSPC)

4401 Wilshire Blvd., 4th Fl., Los Angeles, CA   90010
(323) 556-2550
e-mail: info@horowitzfreedomcenter.org
Web site: www.horowitzfreedomcenter.org

The Center for the Study of Popular Culture (CSPC) is a conservative educational organization that addresses topics such as political correctness, cultural diversity, and discrimination. Its civil rights project promotes equal opportunity for all individuals and provides legal assistance to citizens challenging affirmative action. The center's publishing is centered on two online magazines, *FrontPage Magazine* and *DiscoverTheNetworks.*

Citizens' Commission on Civil Rights (CCCR)

2000 M St. NW, Suite 400, Washington, DC   20036
(202) 659-5565 • fax: (202) 223-5302
e-mail: citizen@cccr.org
Web site: www.cccr.org

The Citizens' Commission on Civil Rights (CCCR) monitors the federal government's enforcement of anti-discrimination laws and promotes equal opportunity for all. It believes that a progressive civil rights agenda benefits all Americans. The commission publishes a variety of articles and reports—many of which are available on their Web site—on both the history of the civil rights movement and current issues facing the civil rights community.

Council of Conservative Citizens
P.O. Box 221683, St. Louis, MO   63122
(636) 940-8474
Web site: www.cofcc.org

The Council of Conservative Citizens believes that the United States is a Christian country, founded by European and Christian peoples. To maintain that heritage, it believes that non-Western immigration must be stopped. The Council promotes its views through its newletter, the *Citizen's Informer*, as well as through a Web site that features news from a white supremacist angle.

Euro-American Issues Forum
PMB 25, San Bruno, CA   94066
(650) 312 8284
e-mail: eaifpres@aol.com
Web site: www.eaif.org

The Euro-American Issues Forum is dedicating to protecting the rights of Americans of European descent. A main activity is the formation of clubs for students of Euroepan descent on high school and college campuses. The organization also publishes reports on race and crime and the *European American Voices* newsletter.

The Heritage Foundation
214 Massachusetts Ave. NE, Washington, DC   20002-4999
(202) 546-4400 • fax: (202) 546-0904
e-mail: info@heritage.org
Web site: www.heritage.org

The Heritage Foundation is a conservative public policy research institute dedicated to free-market principles, individual liberty, and limited government. It opposes affirmative action and believes that the private sector, not government, should be allowed to ease social problems and to improve the status of women and minorities. The foundation publishes the quarterly journal *Policy Review* and the bimonthly newsletter *Heritage Today* as well as numerous books and papers.

National Association for the Advancement of Colored People (NAACP)
4805 Mt. Hope Dr., Baltimore, MD   21215-3297
(410) 580-5777
e-mail: youth@naacpnet.org
Web site: www.naacp.org

The National Association for the Advancement of Colored People (NAACP) is the oldest and largest civil rights organization in the United States. Its principal objective is to ensure the political, educational, social, and economic equality of minorities. It publishes a variety of newsletters, books, and pamphlets, and is associated with the long-running journal *The Crisis*.

Southern Poverty Law Center (SPLC)
400 Washington Ave., Montgomery, AL   36104
(334) 956-8200
Web site: www.splcenter.org

The Southern Poverty Law Center (SPLC) fights discrimination and racism throughout the United States. It has recently turned its attention to promoting immigrants' rights. Its *Intelligence Project* monitors hate groups throughout the United States and reports on individual acts of ethnic or racial violence.

Stormfront
P.O. Box 6637, West Palm Beach, FL   33405
(561) 351-4424
e-mail: comments@stormfront.org
Web site: www.stormfront.org

Stormfront is a white nationalist online community with numerous forums. This organization promotes white superiority and serves as a resource for white political and social action groups. The organization produces a variety of Internet radio shows and hosts a channel for white power music.

U.S. Commission on Civil Rights
624 Ninth St. NW, Suite 500, Washington, DC   20425
(202) 376-7700
e-mail: publications@usccr.gov
Web site: www.usccr.gov

A fact-finding body, the U.S. Commission on Civil Rights reports directly to Congress and the president on the effectiveness of equal opportunity laws and programs. One of its chief tasks is to collect information regarding discrimination. Many of its reports are available on the Web site.

Bibliography

Books

Richard Abanes and Evangeline Abanes — *Homeland Insecurity*. Eugene, OR: Harvest House Publishers, 2007.

Mohamed Adhikari — *Not White Enough, Not Black Enough: Racial Identity in the South African Coloured Community*. Athens: Ohio University Press, 2005.

David Cunningham — *There's Something Happening Here: The New Left, the Klan, and FBI Counterintelligence*. Berkeley: University of California Press, 2004.

Ashley Woody Doane and Eduardo Bonilla-Silva, eds. — *White Out: The Continuing Significance of Racism*. New York: Routledge, 2003.

Abby L. Ferber, ed. — *Home-Grown Hate: Gender and Organized Racism*. New York: Routledge, 2004.

Colin Flint, ed. — *Spaces of Hate: Geographies of Discrimination and Intolerance in the U.S.A.* New York: Routledge, 2004.

Mattias Gardell — *Gods of the Blood: The Pagan Revival and White Separatism*. Durham: Duke University Press, 2003.

Ann Heinrichs	*The Ku Klux Klan: A Hooded Brotherhood.* Chanhassen, MN: Child's World, 2003.
Incite! Women of Color Against Violence	*Color of Violence: The Incite! Anthology.* Cambridge, MA: South End Press, 2006.
Nick Ryan	*Into a World of Hate: A Journey among the Extreme Right.* New York: Routledge, 2004.
Carol M. Swain	*The New White Nationalism in America: Its Challenge to Integration.* New York: Cambridge University Press, 2002.
Gabriel Weimann	*Terror on the Internet: The New Arena, the New Challenges.* Washington, DC: United States Institute of Peace Press, 2006.
George Yancy, ed.	*White on White/Black on Black.* Lanham, MD: Rowman & Littlefield Publishers, 2005.

Periodicals

Josh Adams and Vincent J. Roscigno	"White Supremacists, Oppositional Culture and the World Wide Web," *Social Forces*, December 2005.
Air Force Times	"Extremism in the Military," July 24, 2006.
Autumn Ashante	"White Nationalism Put U in Bondage," *New York Amsterdam News*, March 16, 2006.

Chris Ayres · "Teenage White Supremacists Rock Civil Rights Movement," *Times* (London), October 25, 2005.

Lester Bangs "The White Noise Supremacists," *Village Voice*, April 30, 1979.

Heidi Beirich "Promoting Hate," *Intelligence Report (Southern Poverty Law Center)*, December 2006.

Kathleen M. Blee "Racial Violence in the United States," *Ethnic & Racial Studies*, July 2005.

Sean Cavanagh "Internet Postings Linked to Student Highlight Interest in 'Hate Groups'," *Education Week*, March 30, 2005.

Karen M. Douglas, Craig McGarty, Ana-Maria Bliuc, and Girish Lala "Understanding Cyberhate: Social Competition and Social Creativity in Online White Supremacist Groups," *Social Science Computer Review*, Spring 2005.

Stacy Finz "A Web of White Power," *San Francisco Chronicle*, March 6, 2005.

Andrew Fraser "Adventures of an Academic Pariah," *American Renaissance*, November 2005.

Steve Friess "White-Power Politics," *Newsweek*, August 22, 2005.

David Glen "Can We Improve Race Relations by Giving Racists Some of What They Want?," *Chronicle of Higher Education*, July 19, 2002.

Jacqui Goddard   "Race Row over Club for Whites,"
                        Times Educational Supplement, Octo-
                        ber 3, 2003.

Victor Godinez   "Hate Groups Luring Teens by Mak-
                        ing a Game Out of Racism," *Dallas
                        Morning News*, March 15, 2002.

Michael   "The Political Economy of Identity
MacDonald   Politics," *South Atlantic Quarterly*,
                        Fall 2004.

Alton H. Maddox,   "Is Racial Diversity in America the
Jr.   Cure or the Problem?," *New York
                        Amsterdam News*, July 3, 2003.

Rory McVeigh   "Structured Ignorance and Organized
                        Racism in the United States," *Social
                        Forces*, March 2004.

Andrew Murr and   "White Power, Minus the Power,"
Suzanne Smalley   *Newsweek*, March 17, 2003.

Maureen Murray   "Ex-Supremacist Spreads Anti-
                        Racism," *Toronto Star*, March 21,
                        2002.

Seth Mydans   "African Students' Harsh Lesson:
                        Russian Racism," *New York Times*,
                        December 18, 2003.

Michelle Norris   "Changes in White Supremacist
                        Groups' Leadership May Change the
                        Groups' Public Face," *All Things Con-
                        sidered (NPR)*, August 13, 2003.

Jennifer Ordonez   "The White Album," *Newsweek*, No-
                        vember 7, 2005.

David Oshinsky	"Just Us," *Nation*, February 6, 2006.
Paul Tough	"The Black White Supremacist," *New York Times Magazine*, May 25, 2003.
Steven Weisen-burger	"The Shudder and the Silence: James Baldwin on White Terror," *Anq*, Summer 2002.
Tim Wise	"White Whine: Reflections on the Brain-Rotting Properties of Privilege," *ZNet*, April 20, 2004. www.zmag.org.

Index

A

Affirmative action programs, 27, 56, 57
African Americans, racial identity of, 18–19
American Renaissance (journal), 7, 9, 10
Americans for Legal Immigration Political Action Committee (ALIPAC), 50
Amish, 12–13
Animal rights, 74–75
Anti-Defamation League, 87
Anti-discrimination laws, repeal of, 8
Anti-government activism, 91
Anti-immigrant activists, 42–43, 47–52, 86
Anti-secularism, 90–91
Anti-Semitism, 87–93
Anti-white sentiments, 20, 25
Aryan Nations, 72–73
Aryan race, 48

B

Barkum, Michael, 88
Baumhammers, Richard, 63
Behavior, racial differences in, 21
Belgium
    nationalist parties in, 30–40
    xenophobia in, 36–40
Benfer, Amy, 73
Berlet, Chip, 47
Bible study groups, 75
Biological basis, for race, 18–21, 57

Birth-rate war, 68
Black, Don, 62
Black racial identity, 18–19
Blee, Kathleen, 65
Brimelow, Peter, 9
British National Party, 30
British-Israelism, 88–89
    See also Christian Identity
Burghart, Devin, 51

C

Calabro, Lou, 44–45
California, Hispanic immigration in, 19, 41–46
Change, fear of, 9
Childbearing, 68–69
Children
    care of, as women's responsibility, 72–73
    education of, 10–11, 13–14
    teaching hatred to, 70
Christian Identity, 72, 87–93
Civil rights laws, repeal of, 27
Civil rights movement, 56
Civilization
    clash of, 43
    race and, 21–22
Clinton, Bill, 19
College outreach, 81
Communism, 57
Communities
    building sense of, 100–101
    whites-only, 10–16
Community involvement, 74–75
Council of Conservative Citizens, 63
Courage, 97

Creativity religion, 76–82
Crime, 56, 92–93
Cultural identity, 9
Culture war, 41

D

Demographic shifts, 43–44
Dewinter, Filip, 39–40
Division of labor, gendered, 72–73
Dobbs, Lou, 42
Double standards, 19–20
Douglas, Stephen, 19
D'Souza, Dinesh, 61
Duke, David, 61, 63

E

Eastern Europe, nationalism in, 29–30
Education
    abolition of multiculturalism in, 27
    of children, 10–11, 13–14
    whites-only, 13–14
    See also Schools
Efficacy, 98
Environmentalism, 74–75
Ethnic activist organizations, 7
Europe
    effects of immigration on, 28–35
    immigration to, 8
    nationalist parties in, 29–40
European American Issues Forum (EAIF), 44–45
European cities, decline of, 28–29
Evangelicals, 90
Extremism, nationalist parties promote, 36–40

Extremist groups
    exploitation of immigration issue by, 47–52
    violence promoted by, 87–93
    See also specific groups; White supremacist groups

F

Familial roles, of women, 66–67
Federalism, 26
Flanders, 31–35, 36–40
Foreigners
    hatred of, 38
    See also Immigrants
France, violent clashes in, 29
Francis, Sam, 17, 63
Free Market Party, 63
Freedom High School, 45
Furrow, Buford, 93

G

Gaede, Lamb, 8, 49, 83–86
Gaede, Lynx, 8, 49, 83–86
Giuliani, Rudolph W., 92
Glazov, Jamie, 53
Griffin, Nick, 62
Griffin, Robert, 10, 94

H

Hall, Paul, Jr., 91
Hamm, Mark, 68
Hannity, Sean, 42
Hanson, Victor Davis, 42
Happiness, 98–99
Hate crime laws, repeal of, 27
Hate crimes
    by extremists, 88
    against whites, 44

Hatred
    espoused by white suprema-
        cists, 9
    for foreigners, 38
    recognition of race is not,
        22–23
    spread by Prussian Blue,
        83–86
    teaching of, 70
Hispanic population, whites feel
    threatened by, 41–46
Home schooling, 10–11
Honorable white lifestyle, 94–102
Horowitz, David, 41
Hoskins, Richard Kelly, 93
Huntington, Samuel, 43
Hutchinson, Earl Ofari, 83

I

Identity politics, 55–56
Illegal immigration, crackdown
    on, 26–27
Immigrants
    hatred of, 38
    Muslim, 38–40
Immigration
    ban on, 8, 26
    effects of, in Europe, 28–35
    exploitation of concern over,
        by extremists, 47–52
    Hispanic, in California, 41–46
    impact of, on U.S., 57
    public opinion on, 8–9
    racial segregation and, 55
    uneasiness over, 8–9
Intelligence, racial differences in,
    21
Interracial marriage, 62–63
Islamicisation, fear of, 38–40

J

Jensen, Arthur, 21
Jones, Jim, 12

K

Kagan, Donald, 45–46
Kahl, Gordon, 92
Keillor, Garrison, 99
King, Martin Luther, Jr., 20, 59, 61
Klanswomen, 66–69, 71
Klassen, Ben, 77
Ku Klux Klan (KKK), 48, 51, 61–
    62, 66, 71

L

Latinos. See Hispanic population
Lee, Robert E., 25
Lincoln, Abraham, 19, 53–54
Living white, 94–102
Localism, 26
Lost Tribes, 88–89
Lott, Trent, 19
Lovato, Roberto, 41

M

Marriage, interracial, 62–63
McClelland, Lisa, 45
McVeigh, Timothy, 85, 92
Mennonites, 13
Mental attitude, 98
Mental health, 98
Miles, Robert, 66–67
Militia movement, 91
Militia of Montana, 91
Millenialism, 90
Minorities, protection of racial
    interests by, 24–25
Minority politics, white, 41–42

Minuteman Civil Defense Corps (MCDC), 51
Misogyny, 65
Montana Freemen, 92
Morgan, John Hunt, 10
Mormons, 12
Mugabe, Robert, 25
Multiculturalism
    abandonment of, in schools, 27
    corrosive effect of, 28–29
    national emphasis on, 55–56
Muslim immigrants, fear of, 38–40

N

National Alliance, 49, 50
National Socialist Movement (NSM), 51
National Vanguard, 49–50
Nationalism
    in Eastern Europe, 29–30
    racial, 48–49
Nationalist parties
    Belgian, 30–40
    in Europe, 29–35
    promote xenophobia, 36–40
Nativist sentiments, exploitation of, 47–52
Neo-Nazi groups, 9
    exploitation of immigration issue by, 47–52
    role of women in, 66–69
    See also specific groups
New Century Foundation, 60, 63
Nieli, Russ, 76
Nisbet, Robert, 22

O

Obledo, Mario, 19
Oklahoma City bombing, 92
Orange County, California, 43

O'Reilly, Bill, 42

P

Peoples Temple, 12
Phineas Priesthood, 93
Physical health, 98
Poland, 29–30
Political correctness, 27
Political parties, nationalist, 29–40
Politics
    identity, 55–56
    white minority, 41–42
Populism, 40
Postmillennialism, 90
Potok, Mark, 47–48, 61
Premillennialism, 90
Prussian Blue, 8, 49, 83–86
Pseudo-intellectualism, 59–64
Public opinion, on immigration, 8–9

R

Race
    biological reality of, 18–21, 57
    political reality of, 18–19
    recognition of, 22–23
    significance of, 17–18
Race hatred, 41
Race relations, future of, 57–58
Race riots, in France, 29
Racial consciousness
    need for white, 23–24
    nonwhite, 24–25
Racial differences
    biological, 18–21, 57
    recognizing, is not hate, 22–23
    as source of conflict, 55
Racial domination, problems with, 25
Racial federalism, 26

Racial identity, 18–20, 19–20, 56, 97

Racial integrity, 97

Racial interests, protection of, 24–25

Racial nationalism, 48–49

Racial responsibility, 97

Racial revolution, 22–23

Racial segregation
    advocation of, 7–9
    case for, 53–58
    problems with, 26
    separate communities for, 10–16

Racial survival, 23

Racism
    masking of, by white supremacists, 59–64
    teaching to children, 70
    against whites, 44–45

Reagan, Ronald, 43–44

Right-wing parties, in Europe, 29–40

Robnett, Belinda, 74

Roddy, Dennis, 59

Rogers, Kyle, 28

Roxburgh, Angus, 36

Rudolph, Eric, 92–93

S

Schools
    abolition of multiculturalism in, 27
    importance of, 13–14
    See also Education

Schwarzenegger, Arnold, 44

Self-protection, 24

Self-segregation, 8, 10–16, 26
    See also Racial segregation

Separatism. *See* Racial segregation

Shakers, 12

Sierra Club, 42

Simcox, Chris, 51

Slavery, 25

Smith, Gerald L. K., 89

Social differentiation, 22–23

Socialism, 29

Solidarity, among whites, 17–27

Southern Poverty Law Center, 86

Sovereign citizen movement, 91

Steele, Shelby, 18

Stoddard, Lothrop, 22

Stormfront.org, 49, 50, 62

Strom, Kevin Alfred, 48–49

Student organizations, white, 45

Swift, Wesley, 89

T

Tancredo, Tom, 42

Tate, David, 92

Tax protest movement, 91

Taylor, Jared
    pseudo-intellectualism of, 59–64
    views of, 7–9, 53–58

Temple, Chris, 91

Terrorism, 88, 92

Thurmond, Strom, 19

Tolerance, 39

Toughness, 97

Trask, H. A. Scott, 62

Tribulation, 90

Turner, Hal, 51–52

Turner, Lisa, 76

Two-seed theory, 89–90

Tyndall, John, 62–63

U

United Nuwaubian Nation, 12

United States
    demographic shifts in, 43–44

future of race relations in, 57–58

Hispanic immigrants in, 41–46

impact of immigration on, 57

non-white immigrants in, 8–9

V

Vdare.com, 9

Violence
    encouragement of, 9
    promoted by Christian Identity, 87–93

Vlaams Belang, 31–35

Vlaams Blok, 30–40

W

Western Europe, nationalist parties in, 30–35

White communities, need for, 10–16

White identity
    double standard for, 19–20
    lack of, 18
    need for, 23–24
    rebuilding of, 27

White minority politics, 41–42

White nationalists
    grievances of, 56–57
    message of, 7–9, 53–58
    vs. white supremacists, 53–55

White pride, 8

White student organizations, 45

White supremacist groups
    gendered division of labor in, 72–73
    government and, 85
    leadership roles for women in, 76–82
    new message of, 85–86
    social events of, 70–73

subordinate role of women in, 65–75
    See also specific groups

White supremacists
    exploitation of immigration issue by, 47–52
    mask racism with pseudo-intellectualism, 59–64
    new type of, 7–9
    should lead honorable lives, 94–102
    vs. white nationalists, 53–55

Whites
    disarming of, 24–25
    feel threatened by Hispanics, 41–46
    lack of racial identity for, 18, 56
    as a minority, 9
    must build separate communities, 10–16
    need group solidarity, 17–27
    racism against, 44–45

Wise, Tim, 9

Women
    as bridge from white supremacist groups to outsiders, 73–74
    child care role of, 72–73
    childbearing responsibilities of, 68–69
    community involvement by, 74–75
    familial roles of, 66–67
    leadership roles for, 76–82
    social roles of, 70–72
    subordinate role of, in white supremacist groups, 65–75

World Church of the Creator, 76–82

X

Xenophobia, 9, 36–40

Y

York, Dwight, 12

Z

Zimbabwe, 25